THE MODERN **KNIT** MIX

Vest Bets

30 DESIGNS
TO **KNIT** FOR NOW

THE MODERN **KNIT** MIX

Vest Bets

30

DESIGNS TO **KNIT** FOR NOW

||||||||||||||||||||||||

FEATURING
220 SUPERWASH® ARAN
FROM CASCADE YARNS

sixth&springbooks NEW YORK

sixth&spring books

161 Avenue of the Americas, New York, NY 10013
sixthandspringbooks.com

Editorial Director
JOY AQUILINO

Managing Editor
KRISTY MCGOWAN

Senior Editor
LISA SILVERMAN

Art Director
DIANE LAMPHRON

Project Manager
MICHELLE LO

Page Design
GEMMA WILSON

Yarn Editor
VANESSA PUTT

Editorial Assistant
JOHANNA LEVY

Supervising Patterns Editor
LORI STEINBERG

Patterns Editors
PAT HARSTE
RENEE LORION
MARI LYNN PATRICK
CARLA SCOTT
MARGEAU SOBOTI

Technical Illustrations
LORETTA DACHMAN
RENEE LORION
LORI STEINBERG

Photography
JON MEADE

Hair and Make Up
JENNI DAVIS

Vice President
TRISHA MALCOLM

Publisher
CAROLINE KILMER

Production Manager
DAVID JOINNIDES

President
ART JOINNIDES

Chairman
JAY STEIN

Cataloging-in-Publication Data
Vest bets : 30 designs to knit for now featuring 220 superwash
aran from Cascade Yarns /the editors of Sixth&Spring Books. —
First edition.
    pages cm
ISBN 978-1-936096-81-7
1. Knitting—Patterns. I. Sixth&Spring Books.
TT825.V48 2014
746.43'2041—dc23
                        2014010968

Manufactured in China

1 3 5 7 9 10 8 6 4 2
First Edition

Cascadeyarns.com

Contents

Lovely Layers

How do we love vests? Let us count the ways. First, as the perfect layering piece: no other knitted garment is as versatile or seasonless. A vest can be paired with anything from a button-down oxford to a cotton tee to a feminine, flowery dress. Vests are also a great way to explore innovative and interesting design elements without committing to the time—and quantity of yarn—required for a full sweater.

Style and innovation certainly abound in this book, which includes contributions from beloved knitwear designers such as Nicky Epstein, Deborah Newton, John Brinegar, and Cathy Carron, along with a host of talented up-and-comers. You'll find projects to suit every style and skill level, from simple, modern silhouettes to intricate cables, lace, and colorwork. And all are knitted in Cascade Yarns' 220 Superwash Aran, a brand-new variety of the classic machine-washable wool that brings the same softness, durability, and expansive color palette to an aran-weight yarn.

In the spirit of vests' quick-to-knit nature, and of the book's title, each project is named for a famous racehorse—mostly fillies, of course! We hope this collection will inspire you to add some fun, fashionable vests to your own stable of knits.

Projects

Spring in the Air

Therese Chynoweth starts with a lace body and adds the perfect finishing touch for springtime: an embossed leaf border that is picked up and knit along the curved front and bottom edges.

SIZES
Sized for Small/Medium, X-Large/XX-Large, 1X/2X. Shown in size Small/Medium.

FINISHED MEASUREMENTS
Bust (closed) 36 (42, 48½)"/91.5 (106.5, 123)cm
Length 22¼"/56.5cm

MATERIALS
220 Superwash Aran by Cascade Yarns, 3½oz/100g hanks, each approx 150yd/137.5m (superwash merino wool)
- 5 (6, 7) hanks in #802 green apple
- One size 9 (5.5mm) circular needle, 32"/80cm long, *or size to obtain gauge*
- Stitch holders
- Stitch markers

GAUGE
15 sts and 25 rows to 4"/10cm over lace pat chart using size 9 (5.5mm) needle. *Take time to check gauge.*

SHORT ROW WRAP & TURN (W&T)
On RS row (on WS row)
1) Wyib (wyif), sl next st purlwise.
2) Move yarn between the needles to the front (back).
3) Sl the same st back to LH needle. Turn work. One st is wrapped.

4) When working the wrapped st, insert RH needle under the wrap and work it tog with the corresponding st on needle to close wrap.

3-NEEDLE BIND-OFF

1) Hold right sides of pieces together on 2 needles. Insert 3rd needle knitwise into first st of each needle, and wrap yarn knitwise.
2) Knit these 2 sts together, and slip them off the needles. *Knit the next 2 sts together in the same manner.
3) Slip first st on 3rd needle over 2nd st and off needle. Rep from * in step 2 across row until all sts are bound off.

NOTES

1) The lace pattern is a repeat of 6 stitches plus 3. Follow the lace pattern chart for the vest body.
2) When working the decreases for shaping the armholes and neck, use markers to separate the lace pattern stitch repeats.
3) If a yarn over cannot be worked with its accompanying decrease, work the stitches in Stockinette stitch until there are sufficient stitches for the lace pattern repeat.
4) The embossed leaf border is picked up and knit after the body is complete.

BODY

Cast on 93 (117, 141) sts.
Row 1 (WS) Purl.
Row 2 (RS) Cast on 2 sts, then k1, *yo, ssk, k1, k2tog, yo, k1; rep from *, end yo, ssk, k2.
Row 3 (WS) Cast on 2 sts, purl to end.
Cont in pat st (row 3 of chart) and cast on 2 sts at beg of next 4 rows, then inc 1 st each side every RS row 3 times—111 (135, 159) sts.
Keeping the first and last st in garter st (k every row), work even until piece measures 9½"/24cm from beg.

Divide for Armholes

Next row (RS) Work 19 (25, 31) sts for right front, bind off 4 sts for armhole, work next 65 (77, 89) sts for back, bind off 4 sts for armhole, work to end for left front.

Left Front

Working on 19 (25, 31) sts for left front only, bind off 1 st at beg of next 2 (4, 6) RS rows—17 (21, 25) sts. Work even until armhole measures 4"/10cm.
Armhole inc row (RS) K1, M1, work in pat to end. Rep armhole inc row every 6th row twice more, then every 4th row twice, AT THE SAME TIME, when armhole measures 6½"/16.5cm, dec 1 st at neck edge on next RS row, and place marker (pm) to mark beg of neck decs. Rep neck dec every 4th row twice more. When all shaping is complete, there are 19 (23, 27) sts. Work even until armhole measures 8½"/21.5cm, end with a RS row.

Shape Shoulder

Note Shoulder is shaped using the short row wrap & turn method.
Short row 1 (WS) Work to last 4 (5, 6) sts, w&t. Work to end of row.
Short row 2 (WS) Work to last 9 (11, 13) sts, w&t. Work to end of row.
Short row 3 (WS) Work to last 14 (17, 20) sts, w&t. Work to end of row.
Short row 4 (WS) Work 5 (6, 7) sts, w&t. Work to end of row. Place the 19 (23, 27) sts on a st holder.

Right Front

Rejoin yarn to the right front armhole edge (to beg working next row on the WS) and work as for left front, reversing all shaping. Note that the short row shoulder shaping will beg on a RS (not WS) row.

Back

Rejoin yarn to back armhole edge (to beg working next row on WS) and work armhole as foll: bind off 1 st at beg of next 4 (8, 12) rows—61 (69, 77) sts.

Work even until armhole measures 4½"/11.5cm.
Armhole inc row (RS) K1, M1, work to last st, M1, k1.
Rep inc row every 6th row twice more, then every 4th row twice—71 (79, 87) sts.
Work even until armhole measures 8½"/21.5cm, pm to mark center 23 sts on last WS row.

Shape Neck and Shoulder
Next row (RS) Work to marked sts, join a 2nd ball of yarn and bind off 23 sts, work to last 4 (5, 6) sts, w&t. Cont to work short row shoulder shaping as on left front, AT THE SAME TIME, bind off 3 sts from each neck edge once, then 2 sts once.

FINISHING
Join front and back shoulders using 3-needle bind-off method.

Leaf Border
Beg at left neck edge marker, pick up and k 59 sts along shaped neck edge, pm, 16 sts along curved lower edge, pm, 91 (115, 139) sts along cast-on edge, pm, 16 sts along curved right front edge, pm, 59 sts along right front edge up to neck marker—241 (265, 289) sts.
Note The stitch count will change while working the next 16 rows, as stitches are increased over the curved edges between the markers and bound off at the beginning of rows to shape the neck edges.
Row 1 (WS) Bind off 2 sts, knit to end—239 (263, 287) sts.
Row 2 (RS) Bind off 2 sts, knit to end—237 (261, 285) sts.
Row 3 Bind off 2 sts (1 st on RH needle), k6 more sts, [p1, k5], sl marker (sm), [p1, k1, kfb, k1] 4 times, sm, *p1, k5; rep from * to 1 st before marker, p1, sm, [k1, kfb, k1, p1] 4 times, sm, [k5, p1] 8 times, knit to end—243 (267, 291) sts.
Row 4 Bind off 2 sts, purl 6 more sts, [yo, k1, yo, p5] 8 times, sm, [yo, k1, yo, p4] 4 times, sm, *yo, k1, yo, p5; rep from * to 1 st before marker, yo, k1, yo, sm, [p4, yo, k1, yo] 4 times, sm, [p5, yo, k1, yo] 8 times, purl to end.
Row 5 Bind off 2 sts, knit 4 more sts, [p3, k5] 8 times, sm, [p3, k4] 4 times, sm, *p3, k5; rep from * to 3 sts before marker, p3, sm, [k4, p3] 4 times, sm, [k5, p3] 8 times, knit to end.
Row 6 Bind of 2 sts, purl 4 more sts, [[k1, yo) twice, k1, p5] 8 times, sm, [[k1, yo) twice, k1, p4] 4 times, sm, [[k1, yo) twice, k1, p5] to 3 sts before marker, [k1, yo) twice, k1, sm, [p4, (k1, yo) twice, k1] 4 times, sm, [p5, (k1, yo) twice, k1] 8 times, purl to end.
Row 7 Bind off 2 sts, k2 more sts, [p5, k5] 8 times, sm, [p5, k3, kfb] 4 times, sm, *p5, k5; rep from * to 5 sts before marker, p5, sm, [k3, kfb, p5] 4 times, sm, [k5, p5] 8 times, knit to end.

Row 8 Bind off 2 sts, p2 more sts, *k2, yo, k1, yo, k2, p5; rep from * to last 8 sts and sm, k2, yo, k1, yo, k2, p3.
Row 9 Bind off 2 sts, *p7, k5; rep from * to last 10 sts and sm, p7, k3.
Row 10 Bind off 2 sts, *ssk, k3, k2tog, p5; rep from * to last 8 sts and sm, ssk, k3, p2tog, p1.
Row 11 Sl 1, p2tog, psso, p1, pass dec st over purl st, p2 more sts, [k5, p5] 7 times, k5, sm, [p5, kfb, k4] 4 times, sm, *k5, p5; rep from * to 5 sts before marker, p5, sm, [kfb, k4, p5] 4 times, sm, [k5, p5] 8 times, k1.
Row 12 Sl 1, ssk, psso, k1, pass dec st over knit st, k2tog, [p5, ssk, k1, k2tog] 7 times, p5, sm, [ssk, k1, k2tog, p6] 4 times, sm, *ssk, k1, k2tog, p5; rep from * to 5 sts before marker, ssk, k1, k2tog, sm, [p6, ssk, k1, k2tog] 4 times, sm, [p5, ssk, k1, k2tog] 7 times, p5, ssk, k1.
Row 13 P2tog, k1, pass dec st over, bind off 1 more st, k3, [p3, k5] 7 times, sm, [p3, k6] 4 times, sm, *p3, k5; rep from * to 3 sts before marker, p3, sm, [k6, p3] 4 times, sm, [k5, p3] 7 times, k5, p2.
Row 14 K2tog, p1, pass dec st over, bind off 1 more st, purl 3 more sts, [SK2P, p5] 7 times, sm, [SK2P,

p6] 4 times, sm, *SK2P, p5; rep from * to 3 sts before marker, SK2P, sm, [p6, SK2P] 4 times, sm, [p5, SK2P] 7 times, purl to end.
Row 15 Bind off 2 sts, knit to marker, sm, [k6, kfb] 4 times, sm, knit to marker, sm, k5, [kfb, k6] 3 times, kfb, k1, sm, knit to end.
Row 16 Bind off 2 sts, *k1, p1; rep from * to end for rib, removing markers—243 (267, 291) sts. Bind off all sts in rib.

Neckband
With RS facing, beg at bound-off edge of embossed leaf border on right front, pick up and k 33 sts evenly along right neck, 39 sts along back neck, then 33 sts along left neck—105 sts.
Row 1 (WS) P2tog, *k1, p1; rep from * to last 2 sts for rib, ssp—2 sts decreased.
Row 2 Ssk, work in rib as established to last 2 sts, k2tog—2 sts decreased.
Rep last 2 rows until neckband measures approx ¾"/2cm. Bind off in pat, dec at beg and end of row as established.
Block finished piece to measurements. Ω

STITCH KEY
☐ k on RS, p on WS
⊟ p on RS, k on WS
☒ k2tog
☒ SKP
◙ yo
☒ SK2P

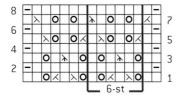

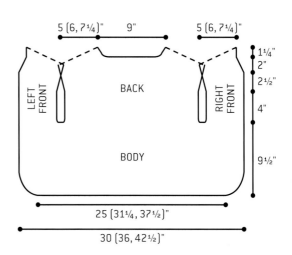

Ruffian

A rustic shade of gray strikes the right tone as **Kathy Zimmerman**
mixes cable motifs to create a winning Aran look.

SIZES
Sized for X-Small, Small, Medium, Large, 1X, 2X.
Shown in size X-Small.

FINISHED MEASUREMENTS
Bust 34 (37, 42, 46, 50, 54)"/86.5 (94, 106.5, 116.5,
127, 137)cm
Length 22½ (22½, 23, 23½, 24½, 25)"/57 (57, 58.5,
59.5, 62, 63.5)cm

MATERIALS
220 Superwash Aran by Cascade Yarns, 3½oz/
100g hanks, each approx 150yd/137.5m
(superwash merino wool)
- 5 (5, 5, 6, 7, 7) hanks in #900 charcoal
- One each sizes 6 and 8 (4 and 5mm) needles
  or size to obtain gauge
- Size 6 (4mm) circular needle, 16"/40cm long
- Cable needle (cn)
- Stitch markers
- Safety pin to hold center st

GAUGE
18 sts and 24 rows to 4"/10cm over rev St st using
larger needles. *Take time to check gauge.*

STITCH GLOSSARY
3-st RPC Sl 2 sts to cn and hold to *back,* k1, p2 from cn.
3-st LPC Sl 1 st to cn and hold to *front*, p2, k1 from cn.
4-st RC Sl 2 sts to cn and hold to *back*, k2, k2 from cn.

4-st LC Sl 2 sts to cn and hold to *front*, k2, k2 from cn.

5-st RPC Sl 3 sts to cn and hold to *back*, k2, sl center st from cn back to LH needle and purl it, k2 from cn.

5-st LPC Sl 3 sts to cn and hold to *front*, k2, sl center st from cn back to LH needle and purl it, k2 from cn.

BACK

With smaller needles, cast on 91 (97, 109, 117, 127, 135) sts.

For size XS only:

Set-up row (WS) K2, p2, *k3, p2; rep from * to last 2 sts, k2.

For sizes S, L, and 1X only:

Set-up row (WS) P2, *k3, p2; rep from * to end.

For size M only:

Set-up row (WS) K1, p2, *k3, p2; rep from * to last st, k1.

For size 2X only:

Set-up row (WS) P1, *k3, p2; rep from * to last 4 sts, k3, p1.

For all sizes:

K the knit sts and p the purl sts for k2, p3 rib, until piece measures 1½"/4cm from beg, end with a WS row. Change to larger needles.

Begin Charts

Row 1 (RS) Work 17 (20, 26, 30, 35, 39) sts in rev St st (p on RS, k on WS), place marker (pm), work chart 1 over 17 sts, chart 2 over 23 sts, chart 3 over 17 sts, pm, work in rev St st to end.

Row 2 (WS) Work in rev St st to marker, sl marker, work chart 3 over 17 sts, chart 2 over 23 sts, chart 1 over 17 sts, work in rev St st to end.

Cont to work charts in this manner, rep rows 1–10 of charts 1 and 3 until row 18 of chart 2 is complete. Cont to rep rows 1–10 of charts 1 and 3 and rep rows 3–18 of chart 2 until piece measures 14 (14, 14, 14, 14½, 14½)"/35.5 (35.5, 35.5, 35.5, 37, 37)cm from beg, end with a WS row.

Shape Armhole

Bind off 5 (5, 6, 6, 8, 8) sts at beg of next 2 rows, 2 (3, 3, 3, 3, 3) sts at beg of next 4 rows, 0 (0, 2, 2, 2, 2) sts at beg of next 0 (0, 2, 2, 4, 6) rows, 1 st at beg of next 8 (8, 8, 10, 12, 14) rows—65 (67, 73, 79, 79, 81) sts.

Work even until armhole measures 7½ (7½, 8, 8½, 9, 9½)"/19 (19, 20.5, 21.5, 23, 24)cm, end with a WS row.

Shape Shoulders

Bind off 5 (6, 6, 7, 7, 7) sts at beg of next 6 (2, 6, 6, 4, 6) rows, then 0 (5, 0, 0, 0, 0) sts at beg of next 0 (4, 0, 0, 0, 0) rows, then 0 (0, 0, 0, 6, 0) sts at beg of next 0 (0, 0, 0, 2, 0) rows. Bind off rem 35 (35, 37, 37, 39, 39) sts for back neck.

FRONT

Work as for back until armhole measures ½ (½, 1, 1½, 2, 2½)"/1.5 (1.5, 2.5, 4, 5, 6.5)cm, end with a WS row. Mark center st.

Shape Neck

Next row (RS) Work in pat to center marked st, place marked st on safety pin to hold, join 2nd ball of yarn and work to end.

Working both sides at once and cont to shape armhole as for front, dec 1 st each neck edge every 4th row once, then every other row 16 (16, 17, 17, 18, 18) times. Work even on 15 (16, 18, 21, 20, 21) sts each side until armhole measures same as back to shoulder. Shape shoulders as for back.

FINISHING

Block pieces to measurements. Sew shoulder and side seams.

Neckband

With RS facing and smaller circular needle, beg at left shoulder, pick up and k 38 sts along left front neck edge, pm, k center st from safety pin, pm, pick up and k 38 sts along right front neck edge, pick up and k 37 (37, 37, 37, 39, 39) sts along back neck—114

(114, 114, 114, 116, 116) sts. Pm for beg of rnd.
Next rnd *P3, k2; rep from * to 3 (3, 3, 3, 4, 4) sts before marker, p3 (3, 3, 3, 4, 4), sl marker, k center st, sl marker, p3 (3, 3, 3, 4, 4), *k2, p3; rep from *, end k2.
Next (dec) rnd Work in rib as established to 2 sts before center st, SKP, sl marker, k1, sl marker, k2tog, work in rib as established to end.
Rep dec rnd 4 times more. Bind off loosely in pat.

Armband

With RS facing and smaller circular needle, beg at underarm, pick up and k 85 (85, 90, 95, 100, 105) sts around armhole opening.
Next rnd *P3, k2; rep from * around for k2, p3 rib.
Work 6 rnds more in rib as established. Bind off. Ω

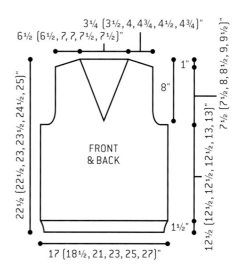

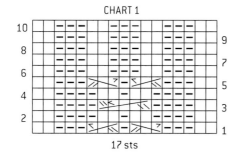

CHART 1
17 sts

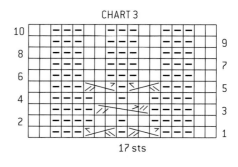

CHART 3
17 sts

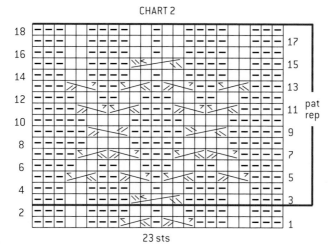

CHART 2
23 sts

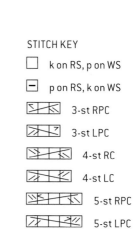

STITCH KEY

☐ k on RS, p on WS

⊟ p on RS, k on WS

3-st RPC

3-st LPC

4-st RC

4-st LC

5-st RPC

5-st LPC

Desert Orchid

The Fair Isle pattern on this design by **Deborah Newton** is both graphic and evocative of nature, and the straight tunic shape will flatter any figure.

SIZES
Sized for Small/Medium, X-Large/XX-Large, 1X/2X. Shown in size Small/Medium.

FINISHED MEASUREMENTS
Bust (closed) 36 (41½, 47)"/91.5 (105.5, 119)cm
Length 26½ (27, 27½)"/67 (68.5, 70)cm

MATERIALS
220 Superwash Aran by Cascade Yarns, 3½oz/100g hanks, each approx 150yd/137.5m (superwash merino wool)
- 2 (3, 3) hanks in #1987 magenta (A)
- 2 (3, 3) hanks in #1988 red plum (B)
- 3 (4, 4) hanks in #875 feather grey (C)
- One each sizes 7, 9, and 10 (4.5, 5.5, and 6mm) circular needle, 40"/102cm long, *or size to obtain gauge*
- Five 1⅛" (27mm) buttons
- Stitch markers

GAUGE
18 sts and 19 rows to 4"/10cm over Fair Isle chart using size 10 (6mm) needle. *Take time to check gauge.*

NOTES
1) Vest is worked back and forth in rows. Circular needle is used to accommodate large number of sts. Do not join.
2) Lower border is worked when body is complete.

BODY
With size 10 (6mm) needle and A, cast on 163 (187, 211) sts.

Begin Fair Isle Chart
Row 1 (RS) Beg where indicated, work row 1 of chart to rep line, then work 24-st rep 6 (7, 8) times across, rep first 10 sts of chart (ending where indicated). Cont to foll chart as established in this way until row 48 is complete. Rep rows 1–48, until piece measures 14¼"/36cm from beg and on the last RS row, work as foll: k41 (47, 53), place marker (pm) for left front; k81 (93, 105), pm for back; k41 (47, 53) for right front.

Divide for Armholes

Next row (WS) [Purl to 6 (8, 10) sts before side seam marker, bind off 6 (8, 10) sts, remove marker, bind off 6 (8, 10) sts] twice, purl to end—35 (39, 43) sts for each front and 69 (77, 85) sts for back. Leave sts on hold for back and left front and work on right front sts only.

Right Front

Work even on 35 (39, 43) sts of right front until armhole measures 5 (5½, 6)"/12.5 (14, 15)cm.

Shape Neck

Next row (RS) Bind off 8 (9, 10) sts, work to end. Cont to shape neck, binding off 3 sts from neck edge twice, then 2 sts twice—17 (20, 23) sts rem. Work even until armhole measures 10 (10½, 11)"/25.5 (26.5, 28)cm.

Shape Shoulder

Bind off 6 (7, 8) sts from shoulder edge twice, then 5 (6, 7) sts once.

Left Front

Return to sts on hold for left front and work shaping as for right front, reversing shaping by binding off for neck on WS rows.

Back

Return to 69 (77, 85) sts on hold for back and join yarn to work next row from RS. Work even on these sts until armhole measures 10 (10½, 11)"/25.5 (26.5, 28)cm, pm on last WS to mark center 15 (17, 19) sts.

Shape Shoulder

Next row (RS) Bind off 6 (7, 8) sts, knit to center marked sts, join a 2nd ball of yarn and bind off center 15 (17, 19) sts, knit to end.
Working both sides at once, bind off 6 (7, 8) sts from each of next 3 shoulder edge rows, then 5 (6, 7) sts from each shoulder once, AT THE SAME TIME, bind off 5 sts from each neck edge twice.

FINISHING

Sew shoulder seams.

Armhole Trim

Note The armhole trim is worked back and forth in rows as a filler, with the straight edges sewn to the armhole bind-offs in the finishing.
With size 9 (5.5mm) needle and C, pick up and k 99 (103, 109) sts evenly along straight edge of armhole. Turn.

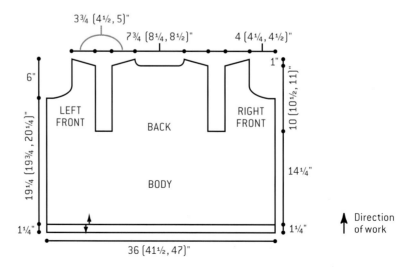

3¾ (4½, 5)"

7¾ (8¼, 8½)"

4 (4¼, 4½)"

1"

6"

10 (10½, 11)"

LEFT FRONT

BACK

RIGHT FRONT

19¼ (19¾, 20¼)"

14¼"

BODY

1¼"

1¼"

Direction of work

36 (41½, 47)"

Row 1 (WS) P2, k1, *p1, k1; rep from * to last 2 sts, p2.
Row 2 (RS) K2, then k the purl sts and p the knit sts to the last 2 sts, end k2.
Rep these 2 rows for 4 (6, 8) rows more. Purl next WS row. Bind off knitwise. Sew edges of trim to fit into armhole bind-offs.

Lower Border

With size 9 (5.5mm) needle and C, from RS, pick up and k 164 (188, 212) sts evenly along lower edge.
Row 1 (WS) P1, k2, *p2, k2; rep from *, end p1.
Row 2 (RS) K1, p2, *k2, p2; rep from *, end k1.
Row 3 P1, p2, *k2, p2; rep from *, end p1.
Row 4 K1, k2, *p2, k2; rep from *, end k1.
Rows 5 and 6 Rep rows 1 and 2. Purl next WS row. Bind off knitwise.

Neckband

With size 7 (4.5mm) needle and C, pick up and k 45 (46, 47) sts from right front neck, 45 (47, 49) sts from back neck, then 45 (46, 47) sts from left front neck edge—135 (139, 143) sts.
Row 1 (WS) P2, k1, *p1, k1; rep from *, end p2.
Row 2 K the knit and p the purl sts.
Rep row 2 for 3 rows more for k1, p1 rib, then change to A and work 1 row more in rib as established. Bind off with A in rib.

Left Front Button Band

With size 7 (4.5mm) needle and B, pick up and k 106 (108, 111) sts along center front edge. Knit 1 row. Change to C and knit 6 rows. Change to A and knit 1 row. Bind off knitwise with A.

Right Front Buttonhole Band

Work as for left front button band for 2 rows.
Buttonhole row (WS) K3, bind off 4 sts, *k16 (17, 17), bind off 4 sts; rep from * 3 times more, knit to end.
Next row Knit, casting on 4 sts over each set of buttonholes. Complete as for left front band.
Sew on buttons to correspond to buttonholes. Ω

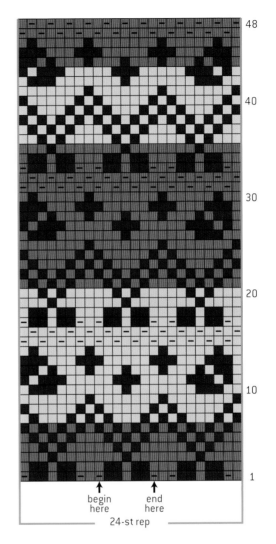

begin here
end here
24-st rep

STITCH KEY
☐ k on RS, p on WS
⊟ p on RS, k on WS

COLOR KEY
▨ A
■ B
☐ C

Belle Marie

Simple lines can be simply stunning, as in this geometric intarsia vest designed by **Cheryl Murray.**

SIZES
Sized for X-Small, Small, Medium, Large, 1X, 2X. Shown in size Small.

FINISHED MEASUREMENTS
Bust 33 (36, 42, 44, 49, 52)"/83.5 (91.5, 106.5, 111.5, 124.5, 132)cm
Length 22 (22½, 23, 23½, 24, 24½)"/56 (57, 58.5, 60, 61, 62)cm

MATERIALS
220 Superwash Aran by Cascade Yarns, 3½oz/100g hanks, each approx 150yd/137.5m (superwash merino wool)
- 1 hank in #893 ruby (A)
- 2 (2, 2, 2, 3, 3) hanks in #815 black (B)
- 2 (2, 2, 2, 3, 3) hanks in #817 aran (C)
- One pair each sizes 8 and 9 (5 and 5.5mm) needles *or size to obtain gauge*
- Size 8 (5mm) circular needle, 16"/40cm long
- Stitch markers

GAUGE
17 sts and 24 rows to 4"/10cm over St st using size 9 (5.5mm) needles. *Take time to check gauge.*

NOTES
1) When changing colors, twist yarns on WS to prevent holes in work.

2) Use a separate bobbin or ball for each color section. Do not carry yarn across back of work.

BACK
With smaller needles and A, cast on 71 (77, 89, 95, 104, 110) sts.
Row 1 (RS) Knit.
Row 2 (WS) K1, *k2, p1; rep from * to last st, k1.
Rep rows 1 and 2 once more.
For sizes XS, S, M, and L only:
Next (dec) row (RS) K1, k2tog, k to end—70 (76, 88, 94) sts.
For all sizes:
Cut A and change to larger needles.
Next row (WS) With C, p35 (38, 44, 47, 52, 55), with B, p35 (38, 44, 47, 52, 55).
Cont in St st and colors as established until piece measures 11"/28cm from beg, end with a WS row. Cut B and C.
Next row (WS) With C, p35 (38, 44, 47, 52, 55), with B, p35 (38, 44, 47, 52, 55).
Cont in St st and colors as established until piece measures 13"/33cm from beg, end with a WS row.

Shape Armhole
Bind off 4 (5, 6, 6, 7, 7) sts at beg of next 2 rows.
Next (dec) row (RS) K1, ssk, k to last 3 sts, k2tog, k1—2 sts dec'd.
Rep dec row every other row 3 (3, 6, 8, 9, 10) times more—54 (58, 62, 64, 70, 74) sts.
Work even until armhole measures 8 (8½, 9, 9½, 10, 10½)"/20.5 (21.5, 23, 24, 25.5, 26.5)cm from beg,

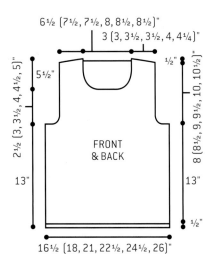

6½ (7½, 7½, 8, 8½, 8½)"

3 (3, 3½, 3½, 4, 4¼)"

5½"

½"

2½ (3, 3½, 4, 4½, 5)"

8 (8½, 9, 9½, 10, 10½)"

FRONT
& BACK

13"

13"

½"

16½ (18, 21, 22½, 24½, 26)"

end with a WS row. Place markers to mark center 26 (30, 30, 32, 34, 34) sts.

Shape Shoulders and Neck
Next row (RS) Bind off 5 (5, 5, 5, 6, 7) sts, work to marker, bind off center 26 (30, 30, 32, 34, 34) sts in color pat, work to end.
Next row Bind off 5 (5, 5, 5, 6, 7) sts, working both sides at once, work to end.
Bind off 4 (4, 5, 5, 6, 6) sts at beg of next 2 rows, AT THE SAME TIME, dec 1 st at each neck edge once.
Bind off rem 4 (4, 5, 5, 5, 6) sts for each shoulder.

FRONT
Work as for back until armhole measures 2½ (3, 3½, 4, 4½, 5)"/6.5 (7.5, 9, 10, 11, 12.5)cm from beg, end with a WS row.

Shape Neck
Next row (RS) With C, k20 (22, 24, 24, 26, 28), bind off center 10 (14, 14, 16, 18, 18) sts in pat, k to end. Working both sides at once, bind off 2 sts at each

neck edge, dec 1 st every other row 7 times, AT THE SAME TIME, when armhole measures same as back to shoulder, shape shoulders as for back.

FINISHING
Block pieces to measurements. Sew shoulder and side seams.

Neckband
With RS facing, circular needle, and A, pick up and k 94 (96, 98, 100, 112, 114) sts around neck edge. Join, place marker for beg of rnd.
Rnd 1 *K1, p2; rep from * around.
Rnd 2 Knit.
Rep rnds 1 and 2 once more, then rep rnd 1 once. Bind off.

Armhole Trim
With RS facing, circular needle and A, pick up and k 74 (78, 82, 86, 90, 94) sts around armhole edge. Join, place marker for beg of rnd. Complete as for neckband. ☊

Dance Smartly

Nicky Epstein gives her open-front ribbed vest a winning twist in the form of striking oversized cables along the front edges and down the center back.

SIZES
Sized for Small/Medium, Large/X-Large, 1X/2X.
Shown in size 1X/2X.

FINISHED MEASUREMENTS
Bust (closed) 39½ (43½, 48)"/100 (110.5, 122)cm
Length (from shoulder to lower edge) 25 (26, 27)"/63.5 (66, 68.5)cm
Note The rib is very elastic, so the piece will fit a wide range of sizes.

MATERIALS
220 Superwash Aran by Cascade Yarns, 3½oz/100g hanks, each approx 150yd/137.5m (superwash merino wool)
- 8 (9, 10) hanks in #893 ruby
- One pair size 9 (5.5mm) needles *or size to obtain gauge*
- One size 9 (5.5mm) double-pointed needle (dpn) or large cable needle (cn)
- Spare size 9 (5.5mm) needle for 3-needle bind-off
- Stitch holders

GAUGE
16 sts and 21 rows to 4"/10cm over eyelet pat, stretched, using size 9 (5.5mm) needles.
Take time to check gauge.

3-NEEDLE BIND-OFF
1) Hold *right* sides of pieces together on 2 needles. Insert 3rd needle knitwise into first st of each needle, and wrap yarn knitwise.
2) Knit these 2 sts together, and slip them off the needles. *Knit the next 2 sts together in the same manner.
3) Slip first st on 3rd needle over 2nd st and off needle. Rep from * in step 2 across row until all sts are bound off.

EYELET RIB
(multiple of 7 sts plus 3)
Row 1 (RS) P3, *k4, p3; rep from * to end.
Row 2 K1, yo, k2tog, *p4, k1, yo, k2tog; rep from * to end.
Rep rows 1 and 2 for eyelet rib.

BACK
Cast on 128 (142, 156) sts.
Row 1 (RS) K5, *P3, k4; rep from * to last 11 sts, p3, k8.
Row 2 P8, *k1, yo, k2tog, p4; rep from * to last 5 sts, p5.
Rep rows 1 and 2 for 6"/15cm, end with a row 2.
Next (cable) row (RS) Work in pat over next 43 (50, 57) sts, sl 21 sts to cn and hold to *front,* work 21 sts in pat, work 21 sts from cn in pat, work to end of row.
Cont in pat, rep cable row every 6"/15cm until piece measures 18"/45.5cm from beg.

Shape Armhole
Bind off 7 sts at beg of next 2 rows, bind off 2 sts at beg of next 2 rows—110 (124, 138) sts.
Cont in pat until armhole measures 7 (8, 9)"/18 (20.5, 23)cm, end with a WS row.
Next (dec) row (RS) K3tog, *p3tog, [k2tog] twice; rep from * to last 2 sts, k2tog (k2tog, k2)—47 (53, 60) sts. Place sts on holder.

LEFT FRONT
Cast on 87 (94, 101) sts.
Work in eyelet rib until piece measures 6"/15cm from beg, end with a WS row.
Next (cable) row (RS) Work in pat over 45 (52, 59) sts, sl 21 sts to cn and hold to *front,* work 21 sts in pat, work 21 sts from cn in pat.
Cont in pat, rep cable row every 6"/15cm until piece measures same as back to armhole, end with a WS row.

Shape Armhole
Bind off 7 sts at beg of next row. Work 1 row even.
Bind off 2 sts at beg of next RS row—78 (85, 92) sts.
Work even until armhole measures 7 (8, 9)"/18 (20.5, 23)cm, end with a WS row.
Next (dec) row (RS) P1, *[k2tog] twice, p3tog; rep from * to last 42 sts, place 16 (19, 22) sts just worked on holder for shoulder, cont in pat on 42 cable sts, working cable row as before until cable measures 3½"/9cm from dec row, end with a WS row.
Next (dec) row (RS) *P3tog, [k2tog] twice; rep from * to end—18 sts. Place sts on holder.

RIGHT FRONT
Cast on 87 (94, 101) sts.
Work in eyelet rib until piece measures 6"/15cm from beg, end with a WS row.
Next (cable) row (RS) Sl first 21 sts to cn and hold to *front,* work 21 sts in pat, work 21 sts from cn in pat, work in pat over 45 (52, 59) sts.
Cont in pat, rep cable row every 6"/15cm until piece measures same as back to armhole, end with a RS row.

Shape Armhole
Bind off 7 sts at beg of next row. Work 1 row even.
Bind off 2 sts at beg of next WS row—78 (85, 92) sts.
Work even until armhole measures 7 (8, 9)"/18 (20.5, 23)cm, end with a RS row.
Next (dec) row (RS) K1, *[p2tog] twice, k3tog; rep from * to last 42 sts, place 16 (19, 22) sts just worked on holder for shoulder, cont in pat on 42 cable sts,

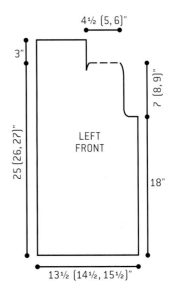

4½ (5, 6)"

3"

7 (8, 9)"

25 (26, 27)"

LEFT
FRONT

18"

13½ (14½, 15½)"

working cable row as before until cable measures
3½"/9cm from dec row, end with a WS row.
Next (dec) row (RS) *P3tog, [k2tog] twice; rep from *
to end—18 sts.

FINISHING

Place back sts on needle, ready to work a RS row.
Place sts for right front shoulder on a 2nd needle,
ready to work a WS row. With spare needle, work
3-needle bind-off over 16 (19, 22) sts to join right
shoulder. Bind off next 15 (15, 16) sts for back neck.
Join left shoulder using 3-needle bind-off.

Collar

Place 18 sts from holders on 2 needles and join, using
3-needle bind-off. Sew edge of collar to back neck. Ω

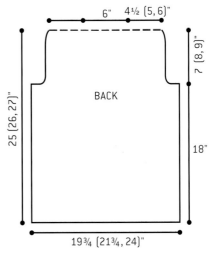

6"   4½ (5, 6)"

7 (8, 9)"

25 (26, 27)"

BACK

18"

19¾ (21¾, 24)"

Rachel Alexandra

The slimming elements in this design by **Cynthia Yanok** include vertical cable and rib panels at the sides and a centered chevron pattern that echoes the V-neck.

SIZES
Sized for Small, Medium, Large, X-Large. Shown in size Small.

FINISHED MEASUREMENTS
Bust 34 (36, 38, 40)"/86 (91.5, 96.5, 101.5)cm
Length 22 (22½, 23, 23½)"/56 (57, 58.5, 59.5)cm

MATERIALS
220 Superwash Aran by Cascade Yarns, 3½oz/100g hanks, each approx 150yd/137.5m (superwash merino wool)
- 4 (4, 5, 5) hanks in #897 baby denim
- One pair each sizes 8 and 10 (5 and 6mm) needles *or size to obtain gauge*
- One each size 8 (5mm) circular needles, 16 and 24"/40 and 60cm long
- Cable needle (cn)
- Stitch holder
- Stitch markers

GAUGES
14 sts and 22 rows to 4"/10cm over chart pat after blocking using larger needles.
One 12-st cable panel is 1¾"/4.5cm wide.
Take time to check gauges.

STITCH GLOSSARY
8-st RC Sl 4 sts to cn and hold to *back*, k4, k4 from cn.

K1, P1 RIB

(over an even number of sts)
Row/rnd 1 (RS) *K1, p1; rep from * to end.
Row/rnd 2 K the knit sts and p the purl sts.
Rep row/rnd 2 for k1, p1 rib.

BACK

With smaller needles, cast on 68 (72, 76, 80) sts.
Work in k1, p1 rib for 1"/2.5cm. Change to larger
needles.

Begin Charts

Row 1 (RS) K4 (5, 6, 7), work chart 1 over 12 sts, k3
(4, 5, 6), work chart 2 over next 30 sts, k3 (4, 5, 6),
work chart 1 over next 12 sts, k4 (5, 6, 7).
Cont to foll charts in this way, rep rows 1–8 of chart 1
until row 14 of chart 2 is complete. Then, cont to work
chart 1 as established and rep rows 7–14 of chart 2
until piece measures 15"/38cm from beg, end with a
WS row.

Shape Armhole

Bind off 2 (3, 3, 4) sts at beg of next 2 rows. Dec 1 st
each side every RS row 2 (2, 3, 3) times—60 (62, 64,
66) sts. Work even until armhole measures 7 (7½, 8,
8½)"/18 (19, 20.5, 21.5)cm, end with a WS row.

Shape Shoulder

Bind off 16 (17, 18, 19) sts at beg of next 2 rows.
Sl rem 28 sts to st holder for back neck.

FRONT

Work as for back until piece measures 13 (13½,
14, 14½)"/33 (34, 35.5, 37)cm from beg, end with
a WS row.

Shape V-Neck

Dec row (RS) Work 32 (34, 36, 38) sts, k2tog, join a
2nd ball of yarn, SKP, work to end. Cont to work both
sides at once, dec 1 st at each neck edge every other
row 3 times more, then every 4th row 10 times, AT THE

SAME TIME, when piece measures 15"/38cm from beg,
work as foll:

Shape Armhole

Bind off 2 (3, 3, 4) sts from each armhole edge once,
then dec 1 st at each armhole edge every RS row 2
(2, 3, 3) times. When all shaping is complete, work
even on 16 (17, 18, 19) sts each side until armhole
measures same as back. Bind off sts each side for
shoulders.

FINISHING

Block pieces to measurements. Sew shoulder seams
and side seams.

Armhole Trim

With shorter circular needle, pick up and k 56 (60,
64, 68) sts evenly around armhole. Join and place
marker (pm) for beg of rnd. Work in rnds of k1, p1 rib
for 1"/2.5cm. Bind off in rib.

Neckband

With longer circular needle, [k1, p1] 14 times across the back neck sts from holder, pick up and k 42 sts along left front edge, pm, pick up and k 1 st at center of V-neck, pm, pick up and k 43 sts along right front neck edge—114 sts. Join and pm to mark beg of rnd.

Rnd 1 Rib to 2 sts before marked center st, k2tog, sl marker, k1, sl marker, SKP, rib to end.

Rnd 2 K the knit sts and p the purl sts.

Rep rnds 1 and 2 until neckband measures 1"/2.5cm. Bind off in rib. Ω

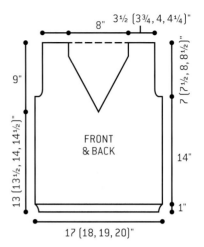

STITCH KEY

☐ k on RS, p on WS

⊟ p on RS, k on WS

8-st RC

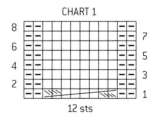

CHART 1

12 sts

CHART 2

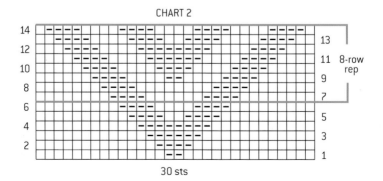

30 sts

Zenyatta

Fiona Ellis combines a mistake-rib stitch with a lace pattern that has strong vertical lines to create a flattering piece that elongates the torso.

SIZES
Sized for X-Small, Small, Medium, Large, X-Large, 1X. Shown in size X-Small.

FINISHED MEASUREMENTS
Bust (closed) 34 (37, 39, 42, 44, 47)"/86 (94, 99, 106.5, 111.5, 119)cm
Length 28½ (29, 29½, 30, 30½, 31)"/72.5 (73.5, 75, 76, 77.5, 78.5)cm

MATERIALS
220 Superwash Aran by Cascade Yarns, 3½oz/100g hanks, each approx 150yd/137.5m (superwash merino wool)
- 6 (6, 7, 8, 8, 9) hanks in #1946 silver grey
- One pair size 9 (5.5mm) needles *or size to obtain gauge*
- Size 9 (5.5mm) circular needle, 40"/162cm long
- One 1⅛"/27mm button
- Stitch markers

GAUGE
19 sts and 26 rows to 4"/10cm over lace or rib pats using size 9 (5.5mm) needles. *Take time to check gauge.*

MISTAKE RIB
(multiple of 6 sts plus 7, plus 2 selvage sts)
Row 1 (RS) K1 (selvage st), p2, *k3, p3; rep from *, end k3, p2, k1 (selvage st).

Row 2 (WS) P1 (selvage st), *p1, k1; rep from *, end p1, p1 (selvage st).
Rep these 2 rows for mistake rib.

BACK
Cast on 81 (87, 93, 99, 105, 111) sts.

Begin Mistake Rib
Work in mistake rib for 16 rows.

Begin Lace Pat Chart
Row 1 (RS) Work first 4 sts of lace pat chart, work 6-st rep 12 (13, 14, 15, 16, 17) times, work last 5 sts of chart. Cont to follow chart in this way until row 18 is complete. Rep these 34 rows for alternating pats until piece measures 20"/51cm from beg.

Shape Armhole
Note While working the armhole and neck shaping, use stitch markers to help maintain the correct number of sts for the paired decrease and yo sts of the lace pat.
Bind off 4 (4, 4, 6, 6, 6) sts at beg of next 2 rows, 3 sts at beg of next 2 rows, 2 sts at beg of next 2 (4, 4, 4, 4, 4) rows. Dec 1 st each side every other row 1 (2, 2, 3, 3, 3) times—61 (61, 67, 67, 73, 79) sts. When all 18 rows of 4th rep of lace pat have been completed, work in mistake rib only (eliminating selvage st on each side) until armhole measures 7½ (8, 8½, 9, 9½, 10)"/19 (20.5, 21.5, 23, 24, 25.5)cm.

Shape Shoulder
Bind off 5 (5, 6, 6, 6, 7) sts at beg of next 4 rows, then 4 (4, 5, 5, 7, 8) sts at beg of foll 2 rows. Bind off rem 33 (33, 33, 33, 35, 35) sts.

LEFT FRONT
Cast on 41 (44, 47, 50, 53, 56) sts.

Begin Mistake Rib Chart
Row 1 (RS) Work first 4 (1, 4, 1, 4, 1) sts of chart, then work 6-st rep 6 (7, 7, 8, 8, 9) times, k1 (selvage st).

Cont to work in mistake rib as established for 15 rows more.

Begin Lace Pat Chart
Row 1 (RS) Work first 4 (1, 4, 1, 4, 1) sts of chart, then work 6-st rep for 6 (7, 7, 8, 8, 9) reps, end k1 (selvage st). Cont to foll chart in this way until row 18 is complete.
Rep these 34 rows for alternating pats until piece measures 20"/51cm from beg.

Shape Armhole and V-Neck
Row 1 (RS) Bind off 4 (4, 4, 6, 6, 6) sts, work to last 3 sts, k2tog (neck dec), k1, pm to mark beg of neck decs.
Row 2 Work even.
Row 3 Bind off 3 sts, work to last 3 sts, k2tog, k1.
Row 4 Work even.
Row 5 Bind off 2 sts, work to last 3 sts, k2tog, k1.
Row 6 Work even.
Cont to bind off 2 sts at beg of next 0 (1, 1, 1, 1, 1) RS rows, then dec 1 st at beg of foll 1 (2, 2, 3, 3, 3) RS rows, AT THE SAME TIME, work neck dec every other row 10 (10, 10, 10, 11, 11) times more, then every 4th row 4 times. Work even on 14 (14, 17, 17, 19, 22) sts until armhole measures same as back.

Shape Shoulder
Bind off 5 (5, 6, 6, 6, 7) sts from shoulder edge twice, then 4 (4, 5, 5, 7, 8) sts once.

RIGHT FRONT
Work as for left front until first 16 rows have been completed in mistake rib.

Begin Lace Pat Chart
Row 1 (RS) K1 (selvage st), work 6-st rep for 6 (7, 7, 8, 8, 9) reps, end with last 4 (1, 4, 1, 4, 1) sts of chart. Then work as for left front, reversing all shaping and working neck dec's on RS rows as foll: k1, ssk, work to end.

FINISHING

Block pieces to measurements. Sew shoulder seams.

Armhole Trim

With size 9 (5.5mm) needles, pick up and k 88 (92, 96, 100, 106, 110) sts evenly around armhole. Knit 1 row. Bind off knitwise. Sew side seams.

Fronts and Neck Trim

With circular needle, beg at lower right front edge, pick up and k 90 sts to neck dec marker, pm on needle, 30 (32, 34, 35, 37, 39) sts to shoulder, 33 (33, 33, 33, 35, 35) sts across back neck, 30 (32, 34, 35, 37, 39) sts to neck dec marker, 90 sts to lower edge—273 (277, 281, 283, 289, 293) sts.

Next row (WS) K to marker on right front, cast on 6 sts for button loop, k to end. Bind off knitwise. Sew on button. ⊙

STITCH KEY

☐ k on RS, p on WS

⊟ p on RS, k on WS

☒ k2tog

☒ SKP

☉ yo

⚄ S2KP

MISTAKE RIB

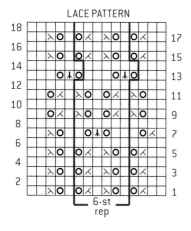

LACE PATTERN

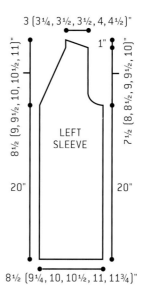

LEFT SLEEVE

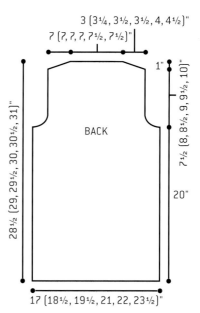

BACK

Lady's Secret

Cathy Carron uses short rows and other clever shaping techniques to create a deceptively simple, decidedly modern, feminine design.

SIZES
Sized for X-Small, Small, Medium, Large. Shown in size Small.

FINISHED MEASUREMENTS
Bust (slightly stretched) 30 (33, 36, 38½)"/ 76 (84, 91.5, 97.5)cm
Length 19 (19½, 20, 20½)"/48 (49.5, 51, 52)cm

MATERIALS
220 Superwash Aran by Cascade Yarns, 3½oz/100g hanks, each approx 150yd/137.5m (superwash merino wool)
- 6 (6, 7, 8) hanks in #1987 magenta
- Size 11 (8mm) circular needle, 29"/40cm long, *or size to obtain gauge*
- Cable needle (cn)
- Stitch markers
- Stitch holders

GAUGE
10 sts and 16 rows to 4"/10cm over St st using size 11 (8mm) needle and 3 strands of yarn held tog.
Take time to check gauge.

NOTE
Vest is worked from the top down, with 3 strands of yarn held together throughout.

BODICE
Neck Edge
With 3 strands of yarn held tog, cast on 92 (96, 100, 104) sts.
Knit 1 row, purl 1 row.
Next row K32 (36, 40, 44), place marker (pm), k30, pm, k30.

Left Front
Next row (RS) K30, turn, leaving rem sts on hold.

Beg Short Row Shaping
Short row 1 (WS) P to last 3 (2, 4, 3) sts, turn, k to end.
Short row 2 (WS) P to 3 (3, 2, 2) sts before previous turn, turn, k to end.
Rep short row 2 until 3 (3, 4, 3) sts rem.
Next row (WS) K30.
Next row (RS) P30.
Rep last 2 rows once more. Bind off knitwise.

Right Front
Join yarn at center front and work next 30 sts for right front as foll:
Row 1 (RS) K30.
Row 2 (WS) P30.
Short row 1 (RS) K to last 3 (2, 4, 3) sts, turn, p to end.
Short row 2 (RS) K to 3 (3, 2, 2) sts before previous turn, turn, p to end.
Rep short row 2 until 3 (3, 4, 3) sts rem.
Next row (RS) P30.
Next row (WS) K30.
Rep last 2 rows once more. Bind off purlwise, do not fasten off.

Back Bodice
Turn work 90 degrees. With RS facing and attached yarn, pick up and k 4 sts across top of right strap (upper edge of border just worked), k 32 (36, 40, 44) sts on hold for back, pick up and k 4 sts across top of left strap—40 (44, 48, 52) sts.
Next row (WS) P4, k2tog, *p1, k1; rep from * to last 4 sts, p3—39 (43, 47, 51) sts.
Next row (RS) K4, p1, *k1, p1; rep from * to last 4 sts, k4.
Cont to work pats in this way until back measures 9"/23cm from cast-on row, end with a RS row. Pm for side seam at end of last row.

Body
Pick up and k 24 (26, 28, 30) sts along lower edge of right front, 1 st at center front, 24 (26, 28, 30) sts along lower edge of left front, pm for beg of rnd—88 (96, 104, 112) sts.
Rnd 1 *P4, k2; rep from * around.
Rep rnd 1 until body measures 10 (10½, 11, 11½)"/25.5 (26.5, 28, 29)cm. Bind off in pat.
Sew edges of neckband at left shoulder. ∩

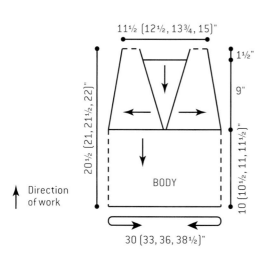

Cicada

Annabelle Speer manages to make a turtleneck silhouette feel light and airy by incorporating wide panels of geometric lace on the front and the back.

SIZES
Sized for Small, Medium, Large, 1X, 2X. Shown in size Small.

FINISHED MEASUREMENTS
Bust 36 (40, 44, 48, 52)"/91.5 (101.5, 111.5, 122, 132)cm
Length 20 (20½, 21, 21½, 22)"/51 (52, 53.5, 54.5, 56)cm

MATERIALS
220 Superwash Aran by Cascade Yarns, 3½oz/100g hanks, each approx 150yd/137.5m (superwash merino wool)
- 6 (7, 8, 9, 10) hanks in #817 aran
- One pair size 10 (6mm) needles *or size to obtain gauge*
- One each sizes 10 and 10½ (6 and 6.5mm) circular needle, 16"/40cm long
- Stitch markers
- Stitch holders

GAUGES
16 sts and 23 rows to 4"/10cm over St st using size 10 (6mm) needles.
15 sts and 23 rows to 4"/10cm over checkerboard mesh st using size 10 (6mm) needles.
Take time to check gauges.

3-NEEDLE BIND-OFF
1) Hold right sides of pieces together on 2 needles. Insert 3rd needle knitwise into first st of each needle, and wrap yarn knitwise.
2) Knit these 2 sts together, and slip them off the needles. *Knit the next 2 sts together in the same manner.
3) Slip first st on 3rd needle over 2nd st and off needle. Rep from * in step 2 across row until all sts are bound off.

CHECKERBOARD MESH STITCH
(multiple of 10 sts plus 4)
Row 1 and all WS rows Purl.
Row 2 (RS) K4, *yo, ssk, k1, [k2tog, yo] twice, k3; rep from * to end.
Row 4 *K3, [yo, ssk] twice, k1, k2tog, yo; rep from * to last 4 sts, k4.
Row 6 K2, *[yo, ssk] 3 times, k4; rep from * to last 2 sts, yo, ssk.
Row 8 K1, *[yo, ssk] 4 times, k2; rep from * to last 3 sts, yo, ssk, k1.
Row 10 Rep row 6.
Row 12 Rep row 4.
Row 14 Rep row 2.
Row 16 K2tog, yo, *k4, [k2tog, yo] 3 times, rep from * to last 2 sts, k2.
Row 18 K1, k2tog, yo, *k2, [k2tog, yo] 4 times, rep from * to last st, k1.
Row 20 Rep row 16.
Rep rows 1–20 for checkerboard mesh st.

BACK

With smaller needles, cast on 70 (78, 86, 94, 102) sts.
Row 1 (RS) K2, *p2, k2; rep from * to end.
Cont in k2, p2 rib as established for 4 rows more.

Beg Checkerboard Mesh St

Row 1 (WS) P13 (17, 21, 25, 29), place marker (pm), work row 1 of checkerboard mesh st over 44 sts, pm, p to end.
Row 2 (RS) K to marker, work row 2 of checkerboard mesh st to marker, k to end.
Cont to work checkerboard mesh st between markers in this way, working sts outside markers in St st, until piece measures 12½"/31.5cm from beg, end with a WS row.

Shape Armholes

Bind off 5 (5, 5, 6, 6) sts at beg of next 2 rows, 2 (3, 4, 4, 5) sts at beg of next 2 rows.
Next row (dec RS) Ssk, work to last 2 sts, k2tog.
Rep dec row every other row 1 (2, 3, 4, 5) times—52 (56, 60, 64, 68) sts.
Work even in pats until armhole measures 7½ (8, 8½, 9, 9½)"/19 (20.5, 21.5, 23, 24)cm, end with a WS row.
Place 12 (14, 15, 16, 17) sts each side on st holders for shoulders, place center 28 (28, 30, 32, 34) sts on st holder for back neck.

FRONT

Work as for back until armhole measures 5½ (6, 6½, 7, 7½)"/14 (15, 16.5, 18, 19)cm, end with a WS row and mark center 18 (18, 20, 22, 24) sts on last row.

Shape Front Neck

Next row (RS) Work to center marked sts, place center 18 (18, 20, 22, 24) sts on st holder, join 2nd ball of yarn and work to end.
Working both sides at once, bind off 2 sts from each neck edge twice, then dec 1 st from each neck edge once—12 (14, 15, 16, 17) sts rem each side.

Work even until armhole measures same as back to shoulder. Place rem sts each side on st holders.

FINISHING

Block pieces lightly to measurements. Join shoulders using 3-needle bind-off.

Neck

With RS facing and smaller circular needle, beg at left shoulder seam, pick up and k 13 sts along shaped left neck edge, k18 (18, 20, 22, 24) from front neck holder, pick up and k 13 sts along shaped right neck edge, k28 (28, 30, 32, 34) from back neck holder—72 (72, 76, 80, 84) sts. Join and pm for beg of rnd.
Rnd 1 *K2, p2; rep from * to end.
Rep rnd 1 until neck measures 4"/10cm. Change to larger circular needle. Rep rnd 1 until neck measures 9"/23cm. Bind off loosely in rib.

Armhole Trim

With RS facing and smaller needles, pick up and k 74 (78, 86, 90, 94) sts evenly along armhole edge.
Row 1 (WS) P2, *k2, p2; rep from * to end.
Cont in k2, p2 rib as established for 4 rows more.
Bind off loosely in rib.
Sew side seams, including armhole trim. Ω

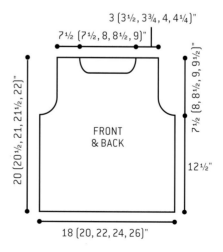

3 (3½, 3¾, 4, 4¼)"

7½ (7½, 8, 8½, 9)"

7½ (8, 8½, 9, 9½)"

20 (20½, 21, 21½, 22)"

FRONT
& BACK

12½"

18 (20, 22, 24, 26)"

Miss Valentine

The cable panels on the back and pockets of this vest designed by **Jill Wright** run in multiple directions, adding a dynamic element to a garment brimming with texture.

SIZES
Sized for Small, Medium, Large, X-Large. Shown in size Small.

FINISHED MEASUREMENTS
Bust 30 (32, 38½, 40½)"/76 (81, 97.5, 103)cm
Length 26"/66cm
Note Bust measurement is given with fronts meeting. When vest is worn open, fit will be more generous.

MATERIALS
220 Superwash Aran by Cascade Yarns, 3½oz/100g hanks, each approx 150yd/137.5m (superwash merino wool)
- 5 (5, 6, 6) hanks in #893 ruby
- One pair size 10 (6mm) needles *or size to obtain gauge*
- Cable needle (cn)
- Stitch markers
- Stitch holders

GAUGES
17 sts and 24 rows to 4"/10cm over moss st using size 10 (6mm) needles.
Chart 2 cable panel = 4½"/11.5cm wide.
Take time to check gauges.

MOSS STITCH
(multiple of 4 sts)
Rows 1 and 2 *K1, p1; rep from * to end.

Rows 3 and 4 *P1, k1; rep from * to end.
Rep rows 1–4 for moss st.

STITCH GLOSSARY
2-st RC Sl 1 st to cn and hold to *back*, k1, k1 from cn.
2-st LC Sl 1 st to cn and hold to *front*, k1, k1 from cn.
4-st RPC Sl 1 st to cn and hold to *back*, k3, p1 from cn.
4-st LPC Sl 3 sts to cn and hold to *front*, p1, k3 from cn.
5-st RPC Sl 2 sts to cn and hold to *back*, k3, p2 from cn.
5-st LPC Sl 3 sts to cn and hold to *front*, p2, k3 from cn.
6-st RC Sl 3 sts to cn and hold to *back*, k3, k3 from cn.
6-st LC Sl 3 sts to cn and hold to *front*, k3, k3 from cn.

NOTES
1) Fronts are made first, then lower back is picked up along left front side edge and worked sideways, then joined to right front side edge. Center back panel is picked up from lower back and worked up, then joined to upper edge of fronts.
2) Note that schematic is drawn with RS of all pieces facing.

POCKET LININGS (MAKE 2)
Cast on 24 sts. Work in moss st for 36 rows. Place sts on st holder.

LEFT FRONT
Cast on 32 (36, 40, 44) sts. Work in moss st for 11 rows.
Row 12 (inc WS) Work 5 (7, 9, 11) sts in pat, M1, [work 2 sts in pat, M1] 11 times, work 5 (7, 9, 11) sts in pat—44 (48, 52, 56) sts.

Begin Charts
Row 1 Work 4 (6, 8, 10) sts in moss st as established, work row 1 of chart 1 over 4 sts, place marker (pm), work row 1 of chart 2 over 28 sts, pm, work row 1 of chart 1 over 4 sts, work 4 (6, 8, 10) sts in moss st as established.
Cont to work pats in this way, working chart 2 through row 26, then working rows 1–10 once more.

Next row (RS) Work 4 (6, 8, 10) sts in moss st, sl next 36 sts to st holder, work in pat across 24 pocket lining sts from holder, work 4 (6, 8, 10) sts in moss st— 32 (36, 40, 44) sts.
Cont in moss st until piece measures 26"/66cm from beg, end with a WS row. Place sts on st holder.

RIGHT FRONT
Work same as for left front.

LOWER BACK
Place markers at side edges of left and right fronts, 4"/10cm and 15¾"/40cm from lower edge.
With RS facing, pick up and k 70 sts along side edge of left front between markers.
Set-up row (WS) P5, [k6, p6, k4, p6, k6, p4] twice, p1.

Begin Charts

Row 1 (RS) K1 (selvage st), [work row 1 of chart 1 over 4 sts, pm, work row 1 of chart 2 over 28 sts, pm] twice, work row 1 of chart 1 over 4 sts, k1 (selvage st).

Cont to work charts in this way, working selvage sts each side in St st, until 26 rows of chart 2 have been worked 3 (3, 4, 4) times, then rep rows 1–10 once more, AT THE SAME TIME, place markers at ends of 25th (25th, 39th, 39th) and 63rd (63rd, 77th, 77th) rows.

Holding pieces so that WS of right front is facing, place lower back between markers at side edge of right front with RS tog. Bind off lower back while joining to right front edge as foll: insert RH needle through edge of right front, then through first lower back st on LH needle, k these 2 sts tog, *insert RH needle through edge of right front, then through next lower back st on LH needle, k these 2 sts tog, pass last st over; rep from * until all sts are bound off and lower back is joined to right front side edge.

CENTER BACK PANEL

With RS facing, pick up and k 38 sts between markers at upper edge of lower back.

Set-up row (WS) P5, k6, p6, k4, p6, k6, p5.

Begin Charts

Row 1 (RS) K1 (selvage st), work row 1 of chart 1 over 4 sts, pm, work row 1 of chart 2 over 28 sts, pm, work row 1 of chart 1 over 4 sts, k1 (selvage st).

Cont to work charts in this way, working selvage sts each side in St st, until 26 rows of chart 2 have been worked twice, then work rows 1–8 (1–6, 1–2, 0) once more.

Join Fronts

Joining row 1 (RS) Sl last 3 sts from right front holder to LH needle, k4tog tbl, work in pat to last st, k last st tog with 3 sts from left front holder for k4tog.

Next row (WS) Work in pat.

Rep last 2 rows 9 (11, 11, 13) times.

For sizes S, L, and XL only:

Joining row 2 Sl 2 sts from right front holder to LH needle, k3tog tbl, work in pat to last st, k last st tog with 2 sts from left front holder for k3tog.

For size L only:

Work 1 row, rep joining row 2 once more.

For all sizes:

Bind off in pat.

FINISHING

Pocket Trim

Place 36 sts from pocket holder on needle.

Join yarn, ready to work a RS row.

Row 1 *K1, p1; rep from * to end.

Cont in k1, p1 rib as established for 3 rows more.

Bind off in pat.

Sew edges of pocket trim to fronts. Sew edges of pocket linings to WS of fronts. Ω

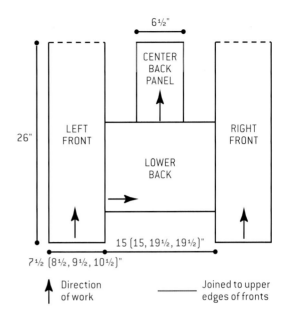

STITCH KEY

☐	k on RS, p on WS
−	p on RS, k on WS
⧖	2-st RC
⧗	2-st LC
	4-st RPC
	4-st LPC
	5-st RPC
	5-st LPC
	6-st RC
	6-st LC

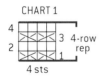

CHART 1

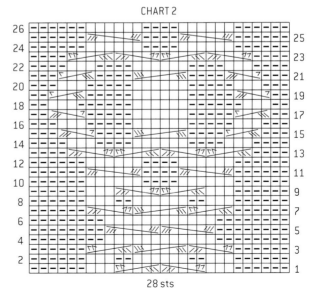

CHART 2

28 sts

Bewitch

Betty Balcolm mixes shades of black, white, and gray for a striking stained glass effect created using elongated slip stitches.

SIZES
Sized for Small, Medium, Large, 1X. Shown in size Medium.

FINISHED MEASUREMENTS
Bust 35¼ (40, 44¾, 49½)"/89.5 (101.5, 113.5, 125.5)cm
Length 25 (26, 26½, 27)"/63.5 (66, 67.5, 68.5)cm

MATERIALS
220 Superwash Aran by Cascade Yarns, 3½oz/100g hanks, each approx 150yd/137.5m (superwash merino wool)
- 3 (3, 4, 4) 3½oz/100g hanks in #815 black (A)
- 1 (1, 2, 2) 3½oz/100g hanks each in #900 charcoal (B), #1946 silver grey (C), and #817 aran (D)
- One each sizes 8 and 9 (5 and 5.5mm) circular needle, 32"/80cm long, *or size to obtain gauge*
- Size 8 (5.5mm) circular needle, 16"/40cm long
- Stitch markers
- Stitch holders

GAUGE
17 sts and 26 rows to 4"/10cm over grid pat using larger needle. *Take time to check gauge.*

STITCH GLOSSARY
PW2 P1, wrapping yarn twice around needle.
KW2 K1, wrapping yarn twice around needle.

3-NEEDLE BIND-OFF
1) Hold right sides of pieces together on 2 needles. Insert 3rd needle knitwise into first st of each needle, and wrap yarn knitwise.
2) Knit these 2 sts together, and slip them off the needles. *Knit the next 2 sts together in the same manner.
3) Slip first st on 3rd needle over 2nd st and off needle. Rep from * in step 2 across row until all sts are bound off.

GRID PATTERN
(worked in rnds, over multiple of 5 sts)
Rnd 1 With A, knit.
Rnd 2 With A, *p4, PW2; rep from * around.
Rnd 3 With B, *k4, sl 1 purlwise, dropping extra wrap; rep from * around.
Rnd 4 With B, *k4, sl 1 purlwise; rep from * around.
Rnds 5 and 6 With B, *k4, sl 1 knitwise; rep from * around.
Rnds 7 and 8 Rep rnds 1 and 2.
Rnds 9–12 With C, rep rnds 3–6.
Rnds 13 and 14 Rep rnds 1 and 2.
Rnds 15–18 With D, rep rnds 3–6.
Rep rnds 1–18 for grid pat in rnds.

GRID PATTERN
(worked back and forth, over multiple of 5 sts plus 4)
Row 1 (RS) With A, knit.
Row 2 (WS) With A, k4, *KW2, k4; rep from * to end.
Row 3 With B, *k4, sl 1 knitwise, dropping extra wrap; rep from * to last 4 sts, k4.

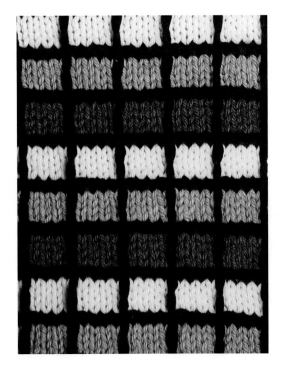

Row 4 With B, p4, *sl 1 purlwise, p4; rep from * to end.

Row 5 With B, *k4, sl 1 knitwise; rep from * to last 4 sts, k4.

Row 6 With B, p4, *sl 1 purlwise, p4; rep from * to end.

Rows 7 and 8 Rep rows 1 and 2.

Rows 9–12 With C, rep rows 3–6.

Rows 13 and 14 Rep rnds 1 and 2.

Rows 15–18 With D, rep rows 3–6.

Rep rows 1–18 for grid pat in rows.

NOTE

Stitches are slipped knitwise or purlwise as indicated, with yarn *always* to the WS of work.

BODY

With longer size 8 (5mm) circular needle and A, cast on 150 (170, 190, 210) sts. Join, taking care not to twist sts, and place marker (pm) for beg of rnd. [K 1 rnd, p 1 rnd] 4 times for garter st. Change to larger needle.

Begin Grid Pat

Work in grid pat in rnds until piece measures 17"/43cm from beg, end with a rnd 6, 12, or 18.

Divide for Front and Back

Next rnd With A, bind off 10 (10, 10, 15) sts, work in pat until there are 54 (64, 74, 74) sts on RH needle for front, bind off 21 (21, 21, 31) sts, knit to end of row. Turn to work back and forth in rows.

Next row (WS) With A, bind off 11 (11, 11, 16) sts, work appropriate row of grid pat in rows over 54 (64, 74, 74) sts for back, place sts for front on st holder.

Back

Working grid pat in rows, cont in pat until armhole measures 8 (9, 9½, 10)"/20.5 (23, 24, 25.5)cm, end with a row 2, 8, or 14, do *not* work double wraps on last row.

Place 14 (19, 24, 24) sts each side on st holders for shoulder, place center 26 sts on st holder for back neck.

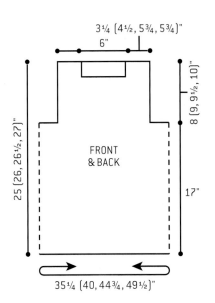

3¼ (4½, 5¾, 5¾)"

6"

8 (9, 9½, 10)"

25 (26, 26½, 27)"

FRONT & BACK

17"

35¼ (40, 44¾, 49½)"

Front

Join A ready to work a WS row. Work as for back until there are 14 rows less than back to shoulder, end with a row 6, 12, or 18.

Shape Front Neck

Next row (RS) With A, k14 (19, 24, 24), turn, leaving rem sts on hold. Work 14 rows in pat. Place sts on hold for left shoulder.

Return to rem sts on hold for front. Leave center 26 sts on st holder for front neck. Join A and work rem 14 (19, 24, 24) sts for right shoulder as for left shoulder. Place sts on hold.

FINISHING

Join shoulders using 3-needle bind-off.

Neck Trim

With RS facing, shorter size 8 (5mm) needle, and A, beg at left shoulder seam, pick up and k 10 sts along left neck edge, k26 from front neck holder, pick up and k 10 sts along right neck edge, k26 from back neck holder—72 sts. Join and pm for beg of rnd.

[K 1 rnd, p 1 rnd] twice. Bind off loosely purlwise.

Armhole Trim

With RS facing, shorter size 8 (5mm) needle, and A, pick up and k 80 (92, 94, 100) sts evenly around armhole edge. Join and pm for beg of rnd.

[K 1 rnd, p 1 rnd] twice. Bind off loosely purlwise. Ω

Rags to Riches

John Brinegar makes a deceptively simple drawstring hoodie a wardrobe must with a modern silhouette and expertly designed finishing.

SIZES
Sized for Small, Medium, Large, 1X, 2X, 3X. Shown in size Small.

FINISHED MEASURMENTS
Bust 34 (38, 42, 46, 50, 54)"/86.5 (96.5, 106.5, 116.5, 127, 137)cm
Length 22½ (23, 23½, 24, 24½, 25)"/57 (58.5, 59.5, 61, 62, 63.5)cm

MATERIALS
220 Superwash Aran by Cascade Yarns, 3½oz/100g hanks, each approx 150yd/137.5m (superwash merino wool)
- 6 (7, 8, 9, 9, 11) hanks in #1994 dusky green
- One each size 8 (5mm) circular needle, 16 and 24"/40 and 60cm long, *or size to obtain gauge*
- Two size 8 (5mm) double-pointed needles (dpns) for I-cord
- Stitch markers
- Stitch holders

GAUGE
18 sts and 24 rows to 4"/10cm over St st using size 8 (5mm) needle. *Take time to check gauge.*

3-NEEDLE BIND-OFF
1) Hold right sides of pieces together on 2 needles. Insert 3rd needle knitwise into first st of each needle, and wrap yarn knitwise.

2) Knit these 2 sts together, and slip them off the needles. *Knit the next 2 sts together in the same manner.
3) Slip first st on 3rd needle over 2nd st and off needle. Rep from * in step 2 across row until all sts are bound off.

I-CORD
With 2 dpns, cast on 4 sts. *Knit one row. Without turning work, slide the sts back to the opposite end of needle to work next row from RS. Pull yarn tightly from the end of the row. Rep from * until desired length. Bind off.

BODY
With longer circular needle, cast on 150 (170, 190, 206, 226, 242) sts. Place marker (pm) for beg of rnd (center back) and join, being careful not to twist sts.
Next rnd K75 (85, 95, 103, 113, 121), pm for center front, k to end.
Work 9 rnds more in St st (k every rnd).
Purl 1 rnd for turning ridge.
Work 4 rnds more in St st.
Next (drawstring hole) rnd K to 2 sts before marker, bind off 4 sts, removing marker, k to end.
Next rnd Knit, casting on 4 sts over bound-off sts. Cont in St st until piece measures 14½"/37cm from turning ridge.
Next rnd K37 (42, 47, 51, 56, 60), pm for side seam, k75 (85, 95, 103, 113, 121), pm for side seam, k to end of rnd.

Shape Armhole

K to first side seam marker, bind off 4 (4, 5, 5, 5, 5) sts, k to next side seam marker, turn to work on sts for front only.

Next row (WS) Bind off 4 (4, 5, 5, 5, 5) sts, p to end.

For sizes 2X and 3X only:

Cont in St st (k on RS, p on WS) and bind off 5 sts at beg of next 2 rows.

For all sizes:

Next (dec) row (RS) K2, k2tog, k to last 4 sts, SKP, k2—2 sts dec'd.

Cont in St st (k on RS, p on WS) and rep dec row every other row 3 (4, 5, 7, 7, 11) times more—59 (67, 73, 75, 77, 77) sts.

Work even until armhole measures 4½ (5, 5½, 6, 6½, 7)"/11 (12.5, 14, 15, 16.5, 18)cm.

Shape Left Neck and Shoulder

Place markers to mark center 11 sts.

K to marker, place 11 sts between markers on st holder, turn.

Next (neck dec) row 1 (WS) P2, p2tog tbl (p2tog tbl, p3tog tbl, p3tog tbl, p3tog tbl, p3tog tbl), p to end.

Rep neck dec row 1 every other row 0 (0, 0, 0, 1, 1) time more. Knit one row.

Next (neck dec) row 2 (WS) P2, p2tog tbl, p to end.

Rep neck dec row 2 every other row 8 times more, AT THE SAME TIME, when armhole measures 7 (7½, 8, 8½, 9, 9½)"/18 (19, 20.5, 21.5, 23, 24)cm, shape shoulders by binding off at beg of RS rows 4 (6, 6, 7, 7, 7) sts, then 4 (6, 7, 7, 7, 7) sts, then 6 (7, 7, 7, 7, 7) sts.

Shape Right Neck and Shoulder

Rejoin yarn to work a RS row, k to end.

Next (neck dec) row 1 (WS) P to last 4 (4, 5, 5, 5, 5) sts, p2tog tbl (p2tog tbl, p3tog tbl, p3tog tbl, p3tog tbl, p3tog tbl), p2.

Rep neck dec row 1 every other row 0 (0, 0, 0, 1, 1) time more. Knit one row.

Next (neck dec) row 2 (WS) P to last 4 sts, p2, p2tog tbl, p to end.

Rep neck dec row 2 every other row 8 times more, AT THE SAME TIME, when armhole measures 7 (7½, 8, 8½, 9, 9½)"/18 (19, 20.5, 21.5, 23, 24)cm, shape shoulders by binding off at beg of WS rows 4 (6, 6, 7, 7, 7) sts, then 4 (6, 7, 7, 7, 7) sts, then 6 (7, 7, 7, 7, 7) sts.

Back

Rejoin yarn to work a RS row.

Shape armholes as for front. Cont in St st until armholes measure same as front to shoulder shaping, end with a WS row.

Shape Shoulders

Bind off 4 (6, 6, 7, 7, 7) sts at beg of next 2 rows, then 4 (6, 7, 7, 7, 7) sts at beg of next 2 rows, then 6 (7, 7, 7, 7, 7) sts at beg of next 2 rows. Bind off rem 31 (31, 33, 33, 35, 35) sts for back neck.

HOOD

Sew shoulder seams.

Leave first 6 sts on holder. Rejoin yarn to k last 5 sts from holder, pick up and k 1 st at beg of neck shaping, pick up and k 16 sts more along right front neck, pick up and k 30 (30, 32, 32, 34, 34) sts along back neck, pick up and k 16 sts along left front neck, k6 from holder—74 (74, 76, 76, 78, 78) sts. Turn.

Next row Purl.

Next row (RS) Cast on 8 sts, k7 for hem, p1 for turning, knit to end, inc 10 sts evenly—92 (92, 94, 94, 96, 96) sts.

Next row (WS) Cast on 8 sts, p7 for hem, k1 for turning, p to last 8 sts, k1, p7—100 (100, 102, 102, 104, 104) sts.

Cont in pat as established for 1"/2.5cm, end with a WS row.

Next (buttonhole) row K7, p1, k3, bind off 2 sts, work to last 13 sts, bind off 2 sts, work in pat to end.

Next row (WS) Work in pat and cast on 2 sts over each buttonhole.

Work even in pat until hood measures 8 (8, 7¾, 7¾, 7½, 7½)"/12.5 (12.5, 19.5, 19.5, 19, 19)cm, end with a WS row. Place marker after first 50 (50, 51, 51, 52, 52) sts.

Shape Hood

Next (dec) row (RS) Work to 3 sts before marker, SKP, k1, sl marker, k1, k2tog, work to end.
Cont in pat, rep dec row every other row 13 (13, 14, 14, 15, 15) times more—72 sts. Divide sts on 2 needles and join top of hood using 3-needle bind-off method.

FINISHING

Armhole Trim

With shorter circular needle, pick up and k 80 (84, 88, 92, 96, 100) sts. Pm for beg of rnd.
Next rnd *K2, p2; rep from * around for k2, p2 rib.
Cont in k2, p2 rib for 4 rnds more. Bind off in pat.

Hood Drawstring

Cast on 4 sts and work I-cord for approx 64"/162.5cm. Place drawstring along WS of hood hem, fold hem over drawstring along turning stitch and sew hem.

Lower Drawstring

Cast on 4 sts and work I-cord for length of bust measurement plus approx 26"/66cm.
Place drawstring along WS of hem, fold hem over drawstring along turning ridge and sew hem. Ω

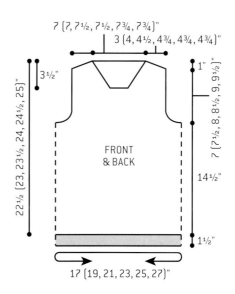

7 (7, 7½, 7½, 7¾, 7¾)"
3 (4, 4½, 4¾, 4¾, 4¾)"
3½"
1"
7 (7½, 8, 8½, 9, 9½)"
22½ (23, 23½, 24, 24½, 25)"
FRONT & BACK
14½"
1½"
17 (19, 21, 23, 25, 27)"

Gallant Bloom

This belted vest designed by **Kathy North** is pure prettiness,
with staggered columns of lace and subtle shaping created by changing needle sizes.

SIZES
Sized for Small, Medium, Large, 1X, 2X, 3X. Shown in size Small.

FINISHED MEASUREMENTS
Bust (closed) 34 (39, 43½, 48½, 52½, 57)"/ 86.5 (99, 110.5, 123, 133.5, 145)cm
Length 33 (33, 34, 34½, 35½, 36)"/84 (84, 86.5, 87.5, 90, 91.5)cm

MATERIALS
220 Superwash Aran by Cascade Yarns, 3½oz/100g hanks, each approx 150yd/137.5m (superwash merino wool)
- 6 (7, 8, 9, 10) hanks in #1988 red plum
- One each sizes 7, 9, and 10½ (4.5, 5.5, and 6.5mm) circular needle, 29"/74cm long, *or size to obtain gauge*
- Size 7 (4.5mm) circular needle, 16"/40cm long
- One pair each sizes 7 and 9 (4.5 and 5.5mm) needles
- Stitch markers

GAUGE
16 sts and 22 rows to 4"/10cm over lace pat st using size 9 (5.5mm) circular needle. *Take time to check gauge.*

NOTES
1) Body of vest is worked in one piece to armholes.
2) Circular needles are used to accommodate larger number of sts. Do not join; work back and forth in rows.
3) Body of vest is shaped by changing needle sizes.
4) When shaping armholes and front necks, work SKP when only one yarn over is possible, or work sts in St st until there are sufficient stitches to work in lace pattern stitch.

SEED STITCH
(over an odd number of sts)
Row/rnd 1 K1, *p1, k1; rep from * to end.
Row/rnd 2 K the purl sts and p the knit sts.
Rep row/rnd 2 for seed st.

BODY
With size 10½ (6.5mm) circular needle, cast on 139 (157, 175, 193, 211, 229) sts. Work in seed st for 10 rows, end with a WS row.
Next row (RS) Work in seed st over first 7 sts, place marker (pm), k to last 7 sts, pm, work in seed st over last 7 sts.
Next row Work in seed st to first marker, sl marker, p to last marker, sl marker, work in seed st over last 7 sts.

Beg Lace Pat Chart
Row 1 (RS) Work in seed st to first marker, sl marker, work first st on chart, work 6-st rep 20 (23, 26, 29, 32, 35) times, work to end of chart, sl marker, work in seed st over last 7 sts. Keeping 7 sts each side in seed st for front borders, cont to foll chart over rem sts through row 20, then rep rows 1–20 for lace pat. Work even until piece measures 12 (12, 12½, 12½,

13, 13)"/30.5 (30.5, 31.5, 31.5, 33, 33)cm from beg, end with a WS row.

Shape Body
Change to size 9 (5.5mm) circular needle. Work even until piece measures 17 (17, 17½, 17½, 18, 18)"/43 (43, 44.5, 44.5, 45.5, 45.5)cm from beg, end with a WS row. Change to size 7 (4.5mm) circular needle and work even until piece measures 19 (19, 19½, 19½, 20, 20)"/48 (48, 49.5, 49.5, 51, 51)cm from beg, end with a WS row. Change to size 9 (5.5mm) needle and work even until piece measures 23 (23, 23½, 23½, 24, 24)"/58.5 (58.5, 59.5, 59.5, 61, 61)cm from beg, end with a WS row.

Divide for Fronts and Back
Next row (RS) Keeping to pat sts as established, work until there are 31 (35, 38, 41, 45, 49) sts on RH needle for right front, bind off next 8 (9, 12, 14, 16, 17) sts, work until there are 61 (69, 75, 83, 89, 97) sts on RH needle for back, bind off next 8 (9, 12, 14, 16, 17) sts, work until there are 31 (35, 38, 41, 45, 49) sts on RH needle for left front.

Left Front
Change to larger straight needles.
Next row (WS) Work in seed st over first 7 sts, sl marker, p24 (28, 31, 34, 38, 42); leave rem sts on circular needle for back and right front.

Shape Armhole and V-Neck
Next row (RS) Bind off first 2 (2, 2, 3, 3, 3) sts, work to end—29 (33, 36, 38, 42, 46) sts. Work next row even.
Dec row 1 (RS) K1, ssk, work to 3 sts before marker, k1, k2tog, sl marker, work in seed st to end. Work next row even. Rep last 2 rows 0 (1, 2, 3, 4, 6) times more—27 (29, 30, 30, 32, 32) sts. Cont to shape V-neck only as foll:
Dec row 2 (RS) Work to 3 sts before marker, k1, k2tog, sl marker, work in seed st to end. Work next row even. Rep last 2 rows 10 (9, 8, 7, 7, 5) times more. Work even on 16 (19, 21, 22, 24, 26) sts until armhole measures 9 (9, 9½, 10, 10½, 11)"/23 (23, 24, 25.5, 26.5, 28)cm, end with a RS row.

Shape Shoulder
At armhole edge, bind off 4 (5, 6, 6, 7, 8) sts once, 4 (5, 6, 6, 7, 7) sts once, then 4 (5, 5, 6, 6, 7) sts once—4 sts.

Neck Extension
Cont in seed st for 3½ (3½, 3½, 3¾, 3¾, 3¾)"/9 (9, 9, 9.5, 9.5, 9.5)cm. Bind off in seed st.

Back
Change to larger straight needles.
Next row (WS) P61 (69, 75, 83, 89, 97).

Shape Armholes
Bind off 2 (2, 2, 3, 3, 3) sts at beg of next 2 rows.
Next (dec) row (RS) K1, ssk, work to last 3 sts, k2tog, k1. Purl next row. Rep last 2 rows 0 (1, 2, 3, 4, 6) times more. Work even on 55 (61, 65, 69, 73, 77) sts until armhole measures same as left front, end with a WS row.

Shape Shoulders

Bind off 4 (5, 6, 6, 7, 8) sts at beg of next 2 rows, 4 (5, 6, 6, 7, 7) sts at beg of next 2 rows, then 4 (5, 5, 6, 6, 7) sts at beg of next 2 rows. Bind off rem 31 (31, 31, 33, 33, 33) sts for back neck.

Right Front

Change to larger straight needles.

Shape Armhole and V-Neck

Next row (WS) Bind off 2 (2, 2, 3, 3, 3) sts, work to end—29 (33, 36, 38, 42, 46) sts.

Dec row 1 (RS) Work in seed st to marker, sl marker, k1, ssk, work to last 3 sts, k2tog, k1. Work next row even. Rep last 2 rows 0 (1, 2, 3, 4, 6) times more—27 (29, 30, 30, 32, 32) sts. Cont to shape V-neck only as foll:

Dec row 2 (RS) Work in seed st to marker, sl marker, k1, ssk, work to end. Work next row even. Rep last 2 rows 10 (9, 8, 7, 7, 5) times more. Work even on 16 (19, 21, 22, 24, 26) sts until armhole measures same as left front, end with a RS row. Shape shoulder and work neck extension as for left front.

BELT

With smaller straight needles, cast on 11 sts. Work even in seed st for 44 (46, 49, 52, 55, 58)"/111.5 (117, 124.5, 132, 139.5, 147)cm (unstretched). Bind off in seed st.

FINISHING

Block piece to measurements. Sew shoulder seams. Sew bound-off edges of neck extensions tog. Sew side edge of neck extension to back neck edge.

Armbands

With RS facing and shorter circular needle, pick up and k 88 (94, 100, 106, 110, 116) sts evenly spaced around armhole edge. Join and pm for beg of rnds. Work around in seed st for 5 rnds. Bind off loosely in seed st. Ω

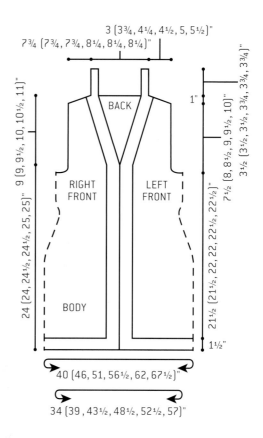

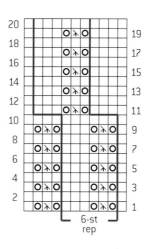

STITCH KEY
☐ k on RS, p on WS
◉ yo
⋏ SK2P

Phar Lap

Flattering diagonal eyelets, crisp I-cord edgings, and
handy belt loops add up to a casually cool design by **Cheryl Murray**.

SIZES
Sized for Small, Medium, Large, 1X, 2X, 3X. Shown in
size Medium.

FINISHED MEASUREMENTS
Bust 33 (36, 41, 45, 48½, 52)"/83.5 (91.5, 104, 114,
123, 132)cm
Length 26 (26½, 27, 27½, 28, 28½)"/66 (67.5, 69.5,
71, 72, 73.5)cm

MATERIALS
220 Superwash Aran by Cascade Yarns, 3½oz/100g
hanks, each approx 150yd/137.5m (superwash
merino wool)
- 4 (4, 5, 5, 6, 6) hanks in #811 teal
- One pair each sizes 8 and 9 (5 and 5.5mm) needles
  or size to obtain gauge
- One each size 9 (5.5mm) circular needles, 16 and
  32"/40 and 80cm long
- Stitch markers

GAUGE
17 sts and 24 rows to 4"/10cm over St st using size 9
(5.5mm) needles. *Take time to check gauge.*

K1, P1 RIB
(over an odd number of sts)
Row 1 (RS) K1, *p1, k1; rep from * to end.
Row 2 (WS) P1, *k1, p1; rep from * to end.
Rep rows 1 and 2 for k1, p1 rib.

I-CORD BIND-OFF
Row 1 *K2, ssk, sl 3 sts from RH needle back to LH
needle, do *not* turn work; rep from * until all sts have
been worked.

EYELET PATTERN 1
(over 6 sts)
Row 1 (RS) K4, k2tog, yo.
Row 2 and all WS rows Purl.
Row 3 K3, k2tog, yo, k1.
Row 5 K2, k2tog, yo, k2.
Row 7 K1, k2tog, yo, k3.
Row 9 K2tog, yo, k4.
Row 10 Purl.
Rep rows 1–10 for eyelet pat 1.

EYELET PATTERN 2
(over 6 sts)
Row 1 (RS) Yo, ssk, k4.
Row 2 and all WS rows Purl.
Row 3 K1, yo, ssk, k3.
Row 5 K2, yo, ssk, k2.
Row 7 K3, yo, ssk, k1.
Row 9 K4, yo, ssk.
Row 10 Purl.
Rep rows 1–10 for eyelet pat 2.

BACK
With smaller needles, cast on 71 (79, 87, 95, 103,
111) sts.
Work in k1, p1 rib for 5 rows.
Change to larger needles.

Beg Eyelet Pats

Set-up row (WS) P15 (19, 23, 27, 31, 35), place marker (pm), p6, pm, p29, pm, p6, pm, p to end.

Row 1 (RS) K to marker, sl marker, work eyelet pat 1 over next 6 sts, sl marker, k to next marker, sl marker, work eyelet pat 2 over next 6 sts, k to end.

Row 2 Purl, slipping markers.

Cont to work in this manner until row 10 of eyelet pats is complete. Rep rows 1 and 2 once more.

Shape Sides

Next (dec) row (RS) K1, ssk, k to last 3 sts, k2tog, k1—2 sts dec'd.

Cont in pats as established, rep dec row every 16th row twice more—65 (73, 81, 89, 97, 105) sts.

Work even until piece measures 11"/28cm from beg, end with a WS row.

Next (inc) row (RS) K1, M1, work to last st, M1, k1—2 sts inc'd.

Rep inc row every 16th row twice more—71 (79, 87, 95, 103, 111) sts.

Work even until piece measures 17"/43cm from beg, end with a WS row.

Shape Armhole

Bind off 6 (6, 6, 7, 7, 8) sts at beg of next 2 rows.

Next (dec) row (RS) K1, k2tog, work to last 3 sts, ssk, k1—2 sts dec'd.

Rep dec row every other row 2 (4, 5, 8, 9, 11) times more—53 (57, 63, 63, 69, 71) sts.

Work even until armhole measures 8 (8½, 9, 9½, 10, 10½)"/20.5 (21.5, 23, 24, 25.5, 26.5)cm from beg, end with a RS row.

Shape Shoulders and Neck

Place markers to mark center 25 (29, 31, 31, 33, 33) sts. Bind off 5 (5, 5, 5, 6, 6) sts at beg of next 2 rows, 4 (4, 5, 5, 6, 6) sts at beg of next 2 rows, AT THE SAME TIME, join a 2nd ball of yarn, bind off center 25 (29, 31, 31, 33, 33) sts, and, working both sides at once, dec 1 st at each neck edge once. Bind off rem 4 (4, 5, 5, 5, 6) sts.

LEFT FRONT

With smaller needles, cast on 35 (39, 43, 47, 51, 55) sts.
Work in k1, p1 rib for 5 rows.
Change to larger needles.

Beg Eyelet Pat 1

Set-up row (WS) P2, pm, p6, pm, p to end.
Row 1 K to marker, sl marker, work eyelet pat 1 over
6 sts, sl marker, k to end.
Row 2 and all WS rows Purl, slipping markers.
Cont to work in this manner until row 10 of eyelet pat
is complete. Rep rows 1 and 2 once more.

Shape Sides

Next (dec) row (RS) K1, ssk, work to end of row—
1 st dec'd.
Rep dec row every 16th row twice more—32 (36, 40,
44, 48, 52) sts.
Work even until piece measures 11"/28cm from beg,
end with a WS row.
Next (inc) row (RS) K1, M1, work to end of row—
1 st inc'd.
Rep inc row every 16th row twice more—35 (39, 43,
47, 51, 55) sts.
Work even until piece measures 16 (16½, 17, 17½,
18, 18½)"/40.5 (42, 43, 44.5, 45.5, 47)cm from beg,
end with a WS row.

Shape Neck

Dec 1 st at neck edge by working k3tog instead of
k2tog in eyelet pat every other row 2 (6, 8, 8, 9, 11)
times, then every 4th row 11 (9, 8, 8, 8, 6) times,
AT THE SAME TIME, when piece measures 17"/43cm
from beg, end with a WS row and shape armhole.

Shape Armhole

Bind off 6 (6, 6, 7, 7, 8) sts at beg of next row.
Next (dec) row (RS) K1, k2tog, work to end of row—
1 st dec'd.
Rep dec row every other row 2 (4, 5, 8, 9, 11) times
more. Work even on rem 13 (13, 15, 15, 17, 18) sts

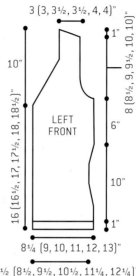

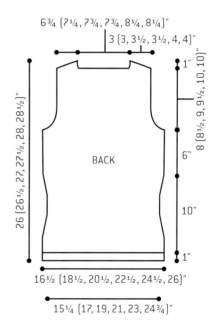

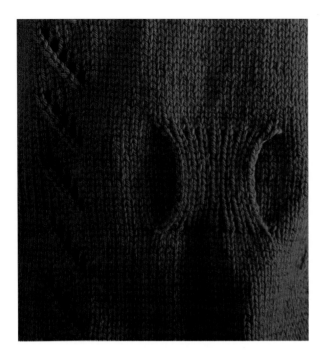

until armhole measures 8 (8½, 9, 9½, 10, 10½)"/
20.5 (21.5, 23, 24, 25.5, 26.5)cm from beg, end with
a WS row. Shape shoulder at armhole edge as for back.

RIGHT FRONT

With smaller needles, cast on 35 (39, 43, 47, 51, 55) sts.
Work in k1, p1 rib for 5 rows.
Change to larger needles.

Beg Eyelet Pat 2

Set-up row (WS) P to last 8 sts, pm, p6, pm, p to end.
Row 1 K to marker, sl marker, work eyelet pat 2 over
6 sts, sl marker, k to end.
Row 2 and all WS rows Purl, slipping markers.
Cont to work in this manner until row 10 of eyelet pat
2 is complete. Rep rows 1 and 2 once more.
Complete to correspond to left front by working side
shaping at end of RS rows, and armhole bind off at beg
of WS rows. Work neck decs in the eyelet pat as SK2P
instead of ssk.

FINISHING

Block pieces to measurements. Sew shoulder and side
seams.

Front and Neck Band

With longer circular needle and RS facing, pick up
and k 102 (104, 106, 108, 110, 112) sts along right
front edge, 24 (30, 32, 32, 34, 34) sts for back neck,
102 (104, 106, 108, 110, 112) sts along left front
edge—228 (238, 244, 248, 254, 258) sts.
Work I-cord bind-off until all sts have been worked.
Bind off rem 3 sts.

Armhole Trim

With shorter circular needle and RS facing, pick up and
k 74 (78, 82, 86, 92, 96) sts around armhole edge.
Join and pm for beg of rnd.
Rnd 1 Cast on 3 sts, work I-cord bind-off to end of rnd.
Cut yarn and thread through rem 3 sts.

Belt Loop

With smaller needles, cast on 17 sts. Work in k1, p1 rib
for 3"/7.5cm. Bind off.
Measure 9½"/24cm from cast-on edge along center
back, pm. Using marker as guide, sew cast-on edge
of belt loop. Sew bound-off edge of belt loop 3"/7.5cm
above. Ω

Ginger Punch

Take the changing seasons in stride in this hooded vest designed by **Sandi Prosser** that features toggle closures, smartly placed diamond cables, and a narrow cable edging.

SIZES
Sized for Small, Medium, Large, 1X, 2X. Shown in size Small.

FINISHED MEASUREMENTS
Bust (closed) 38 (42, 45, 50, 53)"/96.5 (106.5, 114, 127, 134.5)cm
Length 23½ (24, 24½, 25, 26)"/59.5 (61, 62, 63.5, 66)cm

MATERIALS
220 Superwash Aran by Cascade Yarns, 3½oz/ 100g hanks, each approx 150yd/137.5m (superwash merino wool)
- 7 (8, 9, 10, 11) hanks in #822 pumpkin
- One pair size 8 (5mm) needles *or size to obtain gauge*
- Size 8 (5mm) circular needle, 32"/80cm long
- One set (2) size 7 (4.5mm) double-pointed needles (dpns)
- Stitch holders
- Cable needle (cn)
- 5 toggle buttons

GAUGE
18 sts and 25 rows to 4"/10cm over St st using size 8 (5mm) needles. *Take time to check gauge.*

STITCH GLOSSARY

6-st RC Sl 3 sts to cn and hold to *back*, k3, k3 from cn.
4-st RPC Sl 1 st to cn and hold to *back*, k3, p1 from cn.
4-st LPC Sl 3 sts to cn and hold to *front*, p1, k3 from cn.

K2, P2 RIB

(multiple of 4 sts plus 2)
Row 1 (RS) P2, *k2, p2; rep from * to end.
Row 2 K the knit sts and p the purl sts.
Rep row 2 for k2, p2 rib.

K2, P2 RIB

(multiple of 4 sts)
Row 1 (RS) *P2, k2; rep from * to end.
Rep row 1 for k2, p2 rib.

CABLE PANEL

(over 6 sts)
Row 1 (RS) Knit.
Row 2 and all WS rows Purl.
Row 3 6-st RC.
Rows 5 and 7 Knit.
Row 8 Purl.
Rep rows 1–8 for cable panel.

BACK

With size 8 (5mm) needles, cast on 90 (98, 106, 118, 126) sts. Work 4 rows in k2, p2 rib, end with a WS row.
Set-up row (RS) P17 (19, 21, 24, 26), k1, M1, k2, M1, k1, p17 (19, 21, 24, 26), k1, M1, k1, p10, k1, M1, k1, p17 (19, 21, 24, 26), k1, M1, k2, M1, k1, p17 (19, 21, 24, 26)—96 (104, 112, 124, 132) sts.

Beg Chart

Next row (WS) K12 (14, 16, 19, 21), work row 2 of chart over next 16 sts, k12 (14, 16, 19, 21), work row 24 of chart over next 16 sts, k12 (14, 16, 19, 21), work row 2 of chart over next 16 sts, k12 (14, 16, 19, 21).
Next row (RS) P12 (14, 16, 19, 21), work row 3 of chart over next 16 sts, p12 (14, 16, 19, 21), work row 25 of chart over next 16 sts, p12 (14, 16, 19, 21), work row 3 of chart over next 16 sts, p12 (14, 16, 19, 21).
Cont in this manner until row 34 of chart is complete. Work in pats, rep chart rows 3–34, until piece measures 15"/38cm from beg, end with a WS row.

Shape Armhole

Cont in pats as established, bind off 5 (5, 6, 7, 8) sts at beg of next 2 rows. Dec 1 st each side of next RS, then every other row 4 (5, 5, 6, 8) times more—76 (82, 88, 96, 98) sts. Work even in pat until armhole measures 8½ (9, 9½, 10, 10½)"/21.5 (23, 24.5, 25.5, 26.5)cm, end with a WS row.
Next row (RS) Bind off 17 (18, 21, 23, 24) sts, place center 42 (46, 46, 50, 50) sts on holder for back neck, join a 2nd ball of yarn and bind off rem 17 (18, 21, 23, 24) sts.

LEFT FRONT

With size 8 (5mm) needles, cast on 44 (48, 52, 58, 62) sts. Work 4 rows in k2, p2 rib, end with a WS row.
Set-up row (RS) P17 (19, 21, 24, 26), k1, M1, k2, M1, k1, p17 (19, 21, 24, 26), k1, M1, k2, M1, k1, p2—48 (52, 56, 62, 66) sts.

Beg Cable Panel and Chart

Next row (WS) K2, work row 2 of cable panel over next 6 sts, k12 (14, 16, 19, 21), work row 2 of chart over next 16 sts, k12 (14, 16, 19, 21).
Next row (RS) P12 (14, 16, 19, 21), work row 3 of chart over next 16 sts, p12 (14, 16, 19, 21), work row 3 of cable panel over next 6 sts, p2.
Cont in pat as established, rep rows 1–8 of cable panel until row 34 of chart is complete. Cont in pat, rep chart rows 3–34 until piece measures 15"/38cm from beg, end with a WS row.

Shape Armhole

Bind off 5 (5, 6, 7, 8) sts at beg of next row. Work 1 row even in pat. Dec 1 st at end of next RS row, then every

other row 4 (5, 5, 6, 8) times more—38 (41, 44, 48, 49) sts. Work even in pat until armhole measures 6 (6½, 7, 7½, 8)"/15 (16.5, 18, 19, 20.5)cm, end with a WS row.

Shape Neck

Next row (RS) Work to last 15 sts, turn—23 (26, 29, 33, 34) sts. Place rem 15 sts on a st holder for hood. Work 1 row even in pat. Dec 1 st at neck edge every row 3 (5, 5, 7, 7) times, then every other row 3 times more—17 (18, 21, 22, 24) sts. Work even in pat until armhole measures 8½ (9, 9½, 10, 10½)"/21.5 (23, 24.5, 25.5, 26.5)cm, end with a WS row. Bind off rem sts.

RIGHT FRONT

With size 8 (5mm) needles, cast on 44 (48, 52, 58, 62) sts. Work 4 rows in k2, p2 rib, end with a WS row.
Set-up row (RS) P2, k1, M1, k2, M1, k1, p17 (19, 21, 24, 26), k1, M1, k2, M1, k1, p17 (19, 21, 24, 26)—48 (52, 56, 62, 66) sts.

Beg Cable Panel and Chart

Next row (WS) K12 (14, 16, 19, 21), work row 2 of chart over next 16 sts, k12 (14, 16, 19, 21), work row 2 of cable panel over next 6 sts, k2.
Next row (RS) P2, work row 3 of cable panel over next 6 sts, p12 (14, 16, 19, 21), work row 3 of chart over next 16 sts, p12 (14, 16, 19, 21).
Cont in this manner, rep rows 1–8 of cable panel until row 34 of chart is complete. Cont in pats as established, rep rows 3–34 of chart, until piece measures 15"/38cm from beg, end with a RS row.

Shape Armhole

Bind off 5 (5, 6, 7, 8) sts at beg of next row. Dec 1 st at end of next RS row, then every other row 4 (5, 5, 6, 8) times more—38 (41, 44, 48, 49) sts.
Work even in pat until armhole measures 6 (6½, 7, 7½, 8)"/15 (16.5, 18, 19, 20)cm, end with a RS row.

Shape Neck

Next row (WS) Work to last 15 sts, turn—23 (26, 29, 33, 34) sts. Place rem 15 sts on a st holder for hood. Cont in pat, dec 1 st at neck edge *every row* 3 (5, 5, 7, 7) times, then *every other* row 3 times more—17 (18, 21, 23, 24) sts.
Work even in pat until armhole measures 8½ (9, 9½, 10, 10½)"/21.5 (23, 24.5, 25.5, 26.5)cm, end with a WS row. Bind off rem sts.

FINISHING

Block pieces to measurements. Sew shoulder seams.

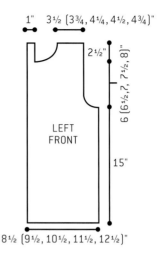

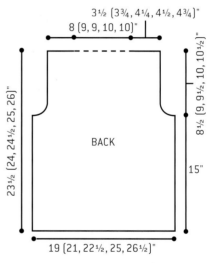

Hood

With RS facing, place 15 sts from right front holder on circular needle. Join yarn and pick up and k 12 sts to shoulder seam, work first 13 (15, 15, 17, 17) sts from back neck holder in pat as established, place marker (pm), work next row of chart across center 16 sts, pm, work rem 13 (15, 15, 17, 17) sts from back neck holder in pat, pick up and k 12 sts evenly along left front neck edge, work across 15 sts from left front holder, next row of cable panel—96 (100, 100, 104, 104) sts.

Row 1 (WS) Work in pat across all sts.

Row 2 (inc row RS) Work to first marker, M1 p-st, sl marker, work to next marker, sl marker, M1 p-st, work to end of row—98 (102, 102, 106, 106) sts. Rep last 2 rows 3 times more—104 (108, 108, 112, 112) sts.

Work even in pat until hood measures 10½"/26.5cm from pick-up row, end with a WS row.

Next (dec) row (RS) Work in pat to 2 sts before first marker, p2tog, sl marker, work to next marker, sl marker, p2tog tbl, work to end of row—102 (106, 106, 110, 110) sts.

Rep dec row every other row 5 times more—92 (96, 96, 100, 100) sts. Work even in pat until hood measures 13"/33cm from pick-up row, end with a WS row. Bind off all sts.

Fold bound-off edge in half and sew top of hood seam.

Armbands

With circular needle and RS facing, pick up and k 96 (102, 108, 112, 118) sts evenly around armhole opening. Work 3 rows in k2, p2 rib. Bind off in rib. Sew side and armband seams.

Front/Hood Edging

With circular needle and RS facing, beg at lower right front edge, pick up and k 338 (346, 358, 366, 382) sts evenly around front and hood edge. Do *not* join, work back and forth in rows. Work 3 rows in k2, p2 rib. Bind off loosely in rib.

I-cord Button Loops (Make 5)

With dpn, cast on 3 sts. *Knit one row. Without turning work, slip sts back to opposite end of needle to work next row from RS. Pull yarn tightly from end of row. Rep from * until I-cord measures approx 3½"/9cm. Bind off knitwise.

Place markers for 5 button loops on right front edge, having the first loop 2"/5cm down from start of neck shaping, the last 2½"/6.5cm from lower edge, and the rem 3 spaced evenly between. Sew I-cord button loops at markers. Sew buttons to left front opposite button loops. Ω

STITCH KEY

☐ k on RS, p on WS

⊟ p on RS, k on WS

6-st RC

4-st RPC

4-st LPC

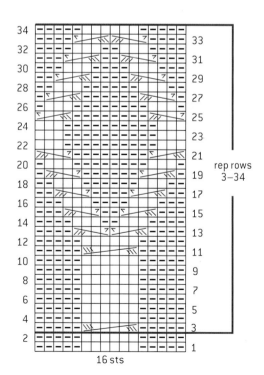

rep rows 3–34

16 sts

Gallorette

Katharine Hunt takes a simple shape and makes it shine with a mosaic pattern in high-contrast colors and a sturdy crocheted edging.

SIZES
Sized for X-Small, Small, Medium, Large, 1X, 2X. Shown in size Small.

FINISHED MEASUREMENTS
Bust (closed) 33 (36½, 40, 44, 47¾, 51½)"/84 (92.5, 101.5, 111.5, 121, 131)cm

Length 21 (21½, 22½, 23, 24, 24½)"/53.5 (54.5, 57, 58.5, 61, 62)cm

MATERIALS
220 Superwash Aran by Cascade Yarns, 3½oz/100g hanks, each approx 150yd/137.5m (superwash merino wool)
- 3 (4, 4, 5, 5, 6) hanks in #813 blue velvet (A)
- 3 (4, 4, 5, 5, 6) hanks in #897 baby denim (B)
- One each sizes 7 and 8 (4.5 and 5mm) circular needle, 29"/74cm long, *or size to obtain gauge*
- Size 7 (4.5mm) circular needle, 16"/40cm long
- One pair size 8 (5mm) needles
- Size E/4 (3.5mm) crochet hook
- Stitch marker

GAUGE
32 sts and 38 rows to 5"/12.5cm over quilted pat st using larger circular needle. *Take time to check gauge.*

SHORT ROW WRAP & TURN (W&T)
On RS row (on WS row)
1) Wyib (wyif), sl next st purlwise.

2) Move yarn between the needles to the front (back).
3) Sl the same st back to LH needle. Turn work. One st is wrapped.
4) When working the wrapped st, insert RH needle under the wrap and work it tog with the corresponding st on needle to close wrap.

K1, P1 RIB

(over an odd number of sts)

Row 1 (RS) K1, *p1, k1; rep from * to end.

Row 2 P1, *k1, p1; rep from * to end.

Rep rows 1 and 2 for k1, p1 rib.

QUILTED PATTERN STITCH

(multiple of 8 sts plus 1)

Set-up row (WS) With A, p1, *p1 wrapping yarn twice around needle, p5, p1 wrapping yarn twice around needle, p1; rep from * to end.

Row 1 (RS) With B, k1, *sl 1 dropping extra wrap, k5, sl 1 dropping extra wrap, k1; rep from * to end.

Row 2 With B, p1, *sl 1, p5, sl 1, p1; rep from * to end.

Row 3 With B, k1, *sl 1, k5, sl 1, k1; rep from * to end.

Row 4 With B, purl, dropping all elongated A slipped sts off needle to back (RS).

Row 5 With A, k1, sl 1, k1, *pick up first dropped st and knit it, k1, pick up next dropped stitch and knit it, then [wyib, sl last 3 sts worked back to LH needle, pass yarn to front, sl same 3 sts back to RH needle, pass yarn to back] twice, k1, sl 3, k1; rep from *, end last rep k1, sl 1, k1 (instead of k1, sl 3, k1).

Row 6 With A, p1, sl 1, *[p1, p1 wrapping yarn twice around needle] twice, p1, sl 3; rep from *, end last rep p1, sl 1, p1 (instead of p1, sl 3).

Row 7 With B, k3, *sl 1 dropping extra wrap, k1, sl 1 dropping extra wrap, k5; rep from *, end last rep k3 (instead of k5).

Row 8 With B, p3, *sl 1, p1, sl 1, p5; rep from *, end last rep p3 (instead of p5).

Row 9 With B, k3, *sl 1, k1, sl 1, k5; rep from *, end last rep k3 (instead of k5).

Row 10 With B, purl, dropping all elongated A slipped sts off needle to back (RS).

Row 11 With A, k1, pick up first dropped st and knit it, k1, sl 3, k1; rep row 5 from * to *, end pick up last dropped st and knit it, k1.

Row 12 With A, p1, *p1 wrapping yarn twice around needle, p1, sl 3, p1, p1 wrapping yarn twice around needle, p1; rep from * to end.

Rep rows 1–12 for quilted pat st.

NOTES

1) Body of vest is made in one piece to armholes.

2) Circular needle is used to accommodate large number of sts. Do not join; work back and forth in rows.

3) Schematic shows measurements after blocking. Work will shorten approximately 1"/2.5cm in total length during blocking. The instructions add an extra ½"/1.3cm to length from bottom edge to underarm and another ½"/1.3cm from underarm to shoulder to accommodate shortening.

4) When working quilted pattern stitch, slip all slipped sts with yarn in back (wyib) on RS rows and with yarn in front (wyif) on WS rows.

BODY

With longer, smaller circular needle, cast on 193 (217, 241, 265, 289, 313) sts. Work in k1, p1 rib for 5 (5, 5, 7, 7, 7) rows, end with a RS row.

Change to larger circular needle.

Work in quilted pat st until piece measures 12½ (12½, 13, 13, 13½, 13½)"/31.5 (31.5, 33, 33, 34, 34)cm from beg, end with a WS row.

Note Piece will measure 12 (12, 12½, 12½, 13, 13)"/30.5 (30.5, 31.5, 31.5, 33, 33)cm after blocking.

Divide for Fronts and Back

Next row (RS) Keeping to quilted pat st, work until there are 37 (42, 47, 52, 57, 62) sts on RH needle (right front), bind off next 14 (16, 18, 20, 22, 24) sts, work until there are 91 (101, 111, 121, 131, 141) sts on RH needle (back), bind off next 14 (16, 18, 20, 22, 24) sts, work until there are 37 (42, 47, 52, 57, 62) sts on RH needle (left front).

Left Front

Change to straight needles. Work next (WS) row even.

Shape Armhole and V-Neck

Dec 1 st from armhole edge on next row, then every other row 5 (5, 6, 8, 10, 12) times more. AT THE SAME TIME, dec 1 st from neck edge on next row, then every 4th row 9 (10, 11, 12, 13, 14) times more. Work even on 21 (25, 28, 30, 32, 34) sts until armhole measures 8½ (9, 9½, 10, 10½, 11)"/21.5 (23, 24, 25.5, 26.5, 28)cm, end with a RS row.

Note Armhole will measure 8 (8½, 9, 9½, 10, 10½)"/20.5 (21.5, 23, 24, 25.5, 26.5)cm after blocking.

Shape Shoulder

Work short row wrap & turn as foll:

Next short row (WS) Work to last 7 (9, 10, 10, 11, 12) sts; w&t. Work to end of row.

Next short row (WS) Work to last 14 (18, 20, 20, 22, 24) sts; w&t. Work to end of row.

Bind off 21 (25, 28, 30, 32, 34) sts, closing wraps as you bind off.

Back

Change to straight needles. Work next row even.

Shape Armholes

Dec 1 st from each armhole edge on next row, then every other row 5 (5, 6, 8, 10, 12) times more. Work even on 79 (89, 97, 103, 109, 115) sts until armhole measures same as left front to shoulder, end with a WS row.

Shape Shoulders

Work short row wrap & turn as foll:

Next 2 short rows Work to last 7 (9, 10, 10, 11, 12) sts; w&t.

Next 2 short rows Work to last 14 (17, 19, 20, 22, 23) sts; w&t.

Next 2 short rows Work to last 21 (25, 28, 30, 32, 34) sts; w&t. Cut yarn. Turn work to RS. Slide sts on RH needle to LH needle. Join A. Using smaller circular needle, bind off all sts, closing wraps as you bind off—21 (25, 28, 30, 32, 34) sts for right back shoulder, 37 (39, 41, 43, 45, 47) sts for back neck, and 21 (25, 28, 30, 32, 34) sts for left back shoulder.

Right Front

Change to straight needles. Work next row even.

Shape Armhole and V-Neck

Work as for left front. Work even on 21 (25, 28, 30, 32, 34) sts until armhole measures same as left front to shoulder, end with a WS row.

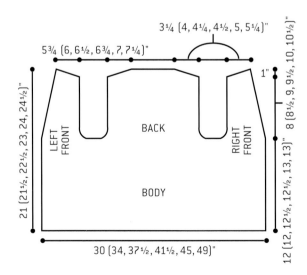

Shape Shoulder

Work short row wrap & turn as foll:

Next short row (RS) Work to last 7 (9, 10, 10, 11, 12) sts; w&t. Work to end of row.

Next short row (RS) Work to last 14 (18, 20, 20, 22, 24) sts; w&t. Work to end of row.

Bind off 21 (25, 28, 30, 32, 34) sts, closing wraps as you bind off.

FINISHING

Block piece to measurements. Sew shoulder seams.

Neckband

With RS facing and crochet hook, join A with a sl st in bottom edge of right front.

Row 1 (RS) Making sure that work lies flat, work 115 (119, 123, 127, 133, 135) sl sts evenly spaced along right front edge to shoulder seam, work 1 st in each of next 37 (39, 41, 43, 45, 47) back neck sts to left shoulder seam, work 115 (119, 123, 127, 133, 135) sl sts evenly spaced along left front edge to bottom edge—267 (277, 287, 297, 311, 317) sts. Fasten off. With RS facing, longer smaller circular needle, and A, pick up and k 1 st in back loop of each sl st—267 (277, 287, 297, 311, 317) sts. Beg with row 2, work in k1, p1 rib for 5 (5, 5, 7, 7, 7) rows. Bind off loosely in rib.

Armbands

With RS facing and crochet hook, skip first 7 (8, 9, 10, 11, 12) sts of underarm bind-off, join A with a sl st in next bound-off st.

Rnd 1 (RS) Making sure work lies flat, work 103 (109, 117, 125, 133, 139) sl sts evenly spaced around entire armhole edge. Join rnd with a sl st in first sl st—104 (110, 118, 126, 134, 140) sl sts. Fasten off. With RS facing, shorter, smaller circular needle, and A, pick up and k 1 st in back loop of each sl st around—104 (110, 118, 126, 134, 140) sts. Place marker for beg of rnd. Work in k1, p1 rib for 5 (5, 7, 7, 7) rnds. Bind off loosely in rib. ◠

Sunline

Tabetha Hedrick shows off a pretty cable-and-rib stitch pattern to best effect with a bright color, adding neutral accents to keep it modern.

SIZES
Sized for Small, Medium, Large, X-Large, 1X, 2X. Shown in size Medium.

FINISHED MEASUREMENTS
Bust (closed) 34 (37, 40, 42, 45, 48)"/86 (94, 101.5, 106.5, 114, 122)cm
Length 23½ (24, 24½, 25, 25½, 26)"/59.5 (61, 62, 63.5, 65, 66)cm

MATERIALS
220 Superwash Aran by Cascade Yarns, 3½oz/100g hanks, each approx 150yd/137.5m (superwash merino wool)
- 5 (5, 6, 6, 7, 7) hanks in #821 daffodil (A)
- 1 hank in #873 extra crème cafe (B)
- One pair size 8 (5mm) needles *or size to obtain gauge*
- One each size 8 (5mm) circular needles, 16" and 24"/40cm and 60cm long
- Cable needle (cn)
- Three ⅞"/22mm buttons

GAUGE
21 sts and 27 rows to 4"/10cm over pat st using size 8 (5mm) needles. *Take time to check gauge.*

STITCH GLOSSARY
2-st LC Sl 1 st to cn and hold to *front,* k1, k1 from cn.
2-st RC Sl 1 st to cn and hold to *back,* k1, k1 from cn.

PATTERN STITCH
(multiple of 4 sts plus 2)
Row 1 (RS) K1, *2-st LC, 2-st RC; rep from *, end k1.
Row 2 K2, * p2, k2; rep from * to end.
Row 3 Knit.
Rows 4 and 5 Rep rows 2 and 3.
Row 6 K1, purl to last st, k1.
Row 7 K1, * 2-st RC, 2-st LC; rep from *, end k1.
Row 8 K2, * p2, k2; rep from * to end.
Row 9 Knit.
Rows 10 and 11 Rep rows 8 and 9.
Row 12 K1, purl to last st, k1.
Rep rows 1–12 for pat st.

K2, P2 RIB
(multiple of 4 sts)
Row 1 (RS) K1, *p2, k2; rep from *, end p2, k1.
Row 2 K3, *p2, k2; rep from *, end k1.
Rep rows 1 and 2 for k2, p2 rib.

BACK
With A, cast on 90 (98, 106, 110, 118, 126) sts.
Rows 1 and 2 Knit.
Row 3 (RS) Knit.
Row 4 K1, purl to last st, k1.
Work in pat st until piece measures approx 16"/40.5cm from beg, end with a row 8.

Shape Armhole
Bind off 7 (7, 7, 7, 9, 9) sts at beg of next 2 rows.
Dec row (RS) K1, ssk, work pat st to last 3 sts, k2tog, k1.

Rep dec row every other row 4 (6, 8, 8, 8, 10) times more—66 (70, 74, 78, 82, 86) sts.
Work even until armhole measures 6¾ (7¼, 7¾, 8¼, 8¾, 9¼)"/17 (18.5, 19.5, 21, 22.5, 23.5)cm.

Shape Shoulder
Bind off 9 (10, 11, 12, 12, 13) sts at beg of next 2 rows, 9 (10, 11, 11, 12, 13) sts at beg of foll 2 rows. Bind off rem 30 (30, 30, 32, 34, 34) sts.

RIGHT FRONT
With A, cast on 58 (62, 66, 70, 74, 78) sts.
Rows 1 and 2 Knit.

Row 3 (RS) Knit.
Row 4 K1, purl to last st, k1.
Then, beg with row 1, work in pat st until piece measures approx 14½"/37cm from beg, end with a row 10.
Next (buttonhole) row (RS) K5, yo, k2tog, work pat st to end.
Rep buttonhole row every 10th (10th, 10th, 10th, 12th, 12th) row twice more, AT THE SAME TIME, when there are same number of rows as back to armhole, end with a RS row and work as foll:

Shape Armhole
Next row (WS) Bind off 7 (7, 7, 7, 9, 9) sts, work to end.
Dec row (RS) Work in pat to last 3 sts, k2tog, k1.
Rep dec row every other row 4 (6, 8, 8, 8, 10) times more—46 (48, 50, 54, 56, 58) sts. Work even until armhole measures 3½ (4, 4½, 5, 5½, 6)"/9 (10, 11.5, 12.5, 14, 15)cm, end with a WS row.

Shape Neck
Next row (RS) Bind off 14 (14, 14, 15, 16, 16) sts, work to end.
Cont to shape neck, binding off 4 (4, 4, 5, 5, 5) sts at beg of next 2 RS rows. Work 1 row even.
Dec row (RS) K1, ssk, work pat st to end. Rep dec row every other row 5 times more—18 (20, 22, 23, 24, 26) sts.
Work even until armhole measures same as back.
Shape Shoulder
Bind off 9 (10, 11, 12, 12, 13) sts from shoulder edge once, then 9 (10, 11, 11, 12, 13) sts once.

LEFT FRONT
With size 8 (5mm) needles and A, cast on 42 (46, 50, 54, 58, 62) sts.
Rows 1 and 2 Knit.
Row 3 (RS) Knit.
Row 4 K1, purl to last st, k1.
Then, beg with row 1, work in pat st until there are same number of rows as back to armhole.

Shape Armhole

Bind off 7 (7, 7, 7, 9, 9) sts at beg of next RS row. Work 1 row even.

Dec row (RS) K1, ssk, work pat st to end. Rep dec row every other row 4 (6, 8, 8, 8, 10) times more—30 (32, 34, 38, 40, 42) sts. Work even until armhole measures 6 (6½, 7, 7½, 8, 8½)"/15 (16.5, 18, 19, 20.5, 21.5)cm, end with a RS row.

Shape Neck

Next row (WS) Bind off 6 (6, 6, 7, 8, 8) sts, work to end.

Dec row (RS) Work in pat to last 3 sts, k2tog, k1. Rep dec row every other row 3 (3, 3, 5, 5, 5) times more, then every 4th row twice—18 (20, 22, 23, 24, 26) sts rem. Work even until armhole measures same as back. Shape shoulder as for right front.

FINISHING

Block pieces to measurements. Sew shoulder and side seams.

Armhole Trims

With shorter circular needle and B, pick up and k 74 (80, 85, 91, 96, 102) sts evenly around armhole. Join and pm to mark beg of rnd. Purl 1 rnd, knit 1 rnd. Bind off purlwise.

Collar

With larger circular needle and B, pick up and k 84 (84, 84, 88, 92, 92) sts evenly around neck edge. Work in k2, p2 rib pat (see stitch glossary) for 24 rows. Bind off loosely in rib.

Right Front Trim

With larger circular needle and B, pick up and k 3 sts for every 4 rows at top of collar. Knit 2 rows. Bind off knitwise. Work left front trim in same way. Sew on buttons to correspond to buttonholes. Ω

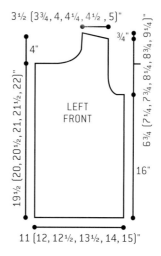

3½ (3¾, 4, 4¼, 4½ , 5)"

¾"

4"

6¾ (7¼, 7¾, 8¼, 8¾, 9¼)"

LEFT FRONT

16"

19½ (20, 20½, 21, 21½, 22)"

11 (12, 12½, 13½, 14, 15)"

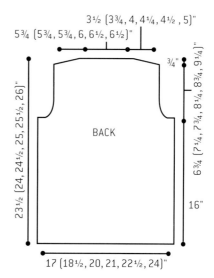

3½ (3¾, 4, 4¼, 4½ , 5)"

5¾ (5¾, 5¾, 6, 6½, 6½)"

¾"

6¾ (7¼, 7¾, 8¼, 8¾, 9¼)"

BACK

23½ (24, 24½, 25, 25½, 26)"

16"

17 (18½, 20, 21, 22½, 24)"

Serena's Song

Patty Lyons cleverly flows a central cable into smaller cables that trace the neckline, with mock cable ribbing at the waist and armbands for a unified design.

SIZES
Sized for Small, Medium, Large, 1X, 2X, 3X. Shown in size Small.

FINISHED MEASUREMENTS
Bust 36 (39, 43, 46, 49, 53)"/91.5 (99, 109, 117, 124.5, 134.5)cm
Length 18 (18½, 19½, 20, 21, 21½)"/45.5 (47, 49.5, 51, 53.5, 54.5)cm

MATERIALS
220 Superwash Aran by Cascade Yarns, 3½oz/100g hanks, each approx 150yd/137.5m (superwash merino wool)
• 4 (5, 6, 6, 7, 7) hanks in #1993 smoke blue
• One pair each sizes 6 and 7 (4 and 4.5mm) needles *or size to obtain gauge*
• Cable needle (cn)
• Stitch markers

GAUGE
24 sts and 36 rows to 5"/12.5cm over St st using larger needles. *Take time to check gauge.*

STITCH GLOSSARY
RT (right twist) K2tog, leaving sts on LH needle; k first st again, sl both sts from needle.
4-st RPC Sl 1 st to cn and hold to *back*, k3, p1 from cn.
4-st LPC Sl 3 sts to cn and hold to *front*, p1, k3 from cn.
6-st RC Sl 3 sts to cn and hold to *back*, k3, k3 from cn.
6-st LC Sl 3 sts to cn and hold to *front*, k3, k3 from cn.
M1 p-st (make 1 purl stitch) Insert LH needle from front to back under strand between last st worked and next st. Purl strand through back loop to twist st.

MOCK CABLE RIB
(multiple of 4 sts plus 2)
Row 1 (RS) P2, *k2, p2; rep from * to end.
Row 2 K2, *p2, k2; rep from * to end.
Row 3 P2, *RT, p2; rep from * to end.
Row 4 Rep row 2.
Rep rows 1–4 for mock cable rib.

BACK
With smaller needles, cast on 86 (94, 102, 110, 118, 126) sts.
Next row (WS) K2, *p2, k2; rep from * to end.
Beg with row 1, cont in mock cable rib for 4 (4¼, 4½, 4½, 5, 5)"/10 (10.5, 11, 11, 12.5, 12.5)cm, end with a RS row. Change to larger needles.
Inc and set-up row (WS) P12 (14, 16, 18, 20, 22), M1 p-st, p10 (11, 12, 13, 14, 15), M1 p-st, p10 (11, 12, 13, 14, 15), place marker (pm), k2, p1, M1 p-st, p1, k4, p6, k4, p1, M1 p-st, p1, k2, pm, p10 (11, 12, 13, 14, 15), M1 p-st, p10 (11, 12, 13, 14, 15), M1 p-st, p12 (14, 16, 18, 20, 22)—92 (100, 108, 116, 124, 132) sts.

Beg Chart 1 and Shape Sides
Beg chart 1 on row 8 (6, 4, 4, 2) and shape sides as foll:
Next (inc) row (RS) K2, M1, k to first marker, sl marker, work row 8 (6, 4, 4, 2, 2) of chart 1 over next 24 sts, sl marker, k to last 2 sts, M1, k2—94 (102,

110, 118, 126, 134) sts. Cont to foll chart 1 through row 28, then rep rows 5–25, end with a WS row—42 (44, 46, 46, 48, 48) rows completed. AT THE SAME TIME, working each side of markers in St st, cont to inc 1 st each side every 8th row twice more—98 (106, 114, 122, 130, 138) sts.

Divide and Shape V-Neck

Next (set-up and dec) row (RS) K to first marker, sl marker, p2, p2tog, k6, p2; join a 2nd ball of yarn, p2, k6, p2tog, p2, sl marker, k to end—48 (52, 56, 60, 64, 68) sts each side.

Next row K the knit sts and p the purl sts.

Next (set-up and dec) row (RS) With first ball of yarn, k to marker, sl marker, p1, p2tog, k6, p2; with 2nd ball of yarn, p2, k6, p2tog, p1, sl marker, k to end—47 (51, 55, 59, 63, 67) sts each side.

Next row K the knit sts and p the purl sts.

Beg Charts 2 and 3

Beg charts on row 3 and cont to shape V-neck as foll:

Row (dec) (RS) With first ball of yarn, k to 3 sts before marker, ssk, k1, sl marker, work chart 2 over next 10

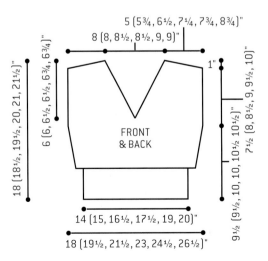

sts; with 2nd ball of yarn, work chart 3 over next 10 sts, sl marker, k1, k2tog, k to end—46 (50, 54, 58, 62, 66) sts each side. Cont to foll charts through row 6, then rep rows 1–6 for cable pats. AT THE SAME TIME, cont to dec 1 st along each neck edge every other row 18 (18, 19, 19, 20, 20) times more. Work even on 28 (32, 35, 39, 42, 46) sts each side until piece measures 17 (17½, 18½, 19, 20, 20½)"/43 (44.5, 47, 48, 51, 52)cm from beg, end with a WS row.

Shape Shoulders

Bind off 10 (11, 12, 13, 14, 16) sts at beg of next 2 rows, 9 (11, 12, 13, 14, 15) sts at beg of next 2 rows, then 9 (10, 11, 13, 14, 15) sts at beg of next 2 rows.

FRONT

Work as for back.

FINISHING

Block pieces to measurements. Sew shoulder seams. Place markers 7½ (8, 8½, 9, 9½, 10)"/19 (20.5, 21.5, 23, 24, 25.5)cm down from shoulders on back and front.

Armbands

With RS facing and smaller needles, pick up and k 90 (98, 106, 110, 114, 122) sts evenly spaced along armhole edge. Beg with row 2 (WS), work in mock cable rib through row 4, then rep rows 1–3 once more, end with a RS row. Bind off loosely in rib. Sew side and armband seams. ∩

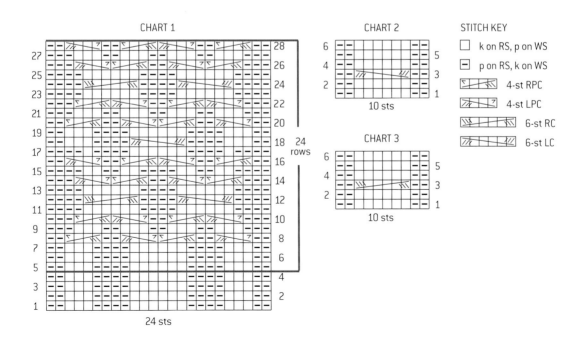

CHART 1
24 sts
24 rows

CHART 2
10 sts

CHART 3
10 sts

STITCH KEY

☐ k on RS, p on WS

⊟ p on RS, k on WS

4-st RPC

4-st LPC

6-st RC

6-st LC

Dahlia

Pat Olski adds flair to a stockinette vest with oversized cable panels extending past the bottom edge into a single, striking leaf motif.

SIZES
Sized for Small, Medium, Large. Shown in size Small.

FINISHED MEASUREMENTS
Bust (closed) 36 (39, 43)"/91.5 (99, 109)cm
Length 24 (24½, 25)"/61 (62, 63.5)cm

MATERIALS
220 Superwash Aran by Cascade Yarns, 3½oz/100g hanks, each approx 150yd/137.5m (superwash merino wool)
- 5 (6, 7) hanks in #875 feather grey
- One pair each sizes 6 and 8 (4 and 5mm) needles *or size to obtain gauge*
- Spare size 8 (5mm) needle
- Cable needle (cn)
- Stitch markers
- Two medium hook-and-eye sets

GAUGE
18 sts and 24 rows to 4"/10cm over St st using size larger needles. *Take time to check gauge.*

STITCH GLOSSARY
5-st RPC Sl 1 st to cn and hold to *back,* k4, p1 from cn.
5-st LPC Sl 4 sts to cn and hold to *front,* p1, k4 from cn.
6-st RPC Sl 2 sts to cn and hold to *back,* k4, p2 from cn.
6-st LPC Sl 4 sts to cn and hold to *front,* p2, k4 from cn.
8-st RC Sl 4 sts to cn and hold to *back,* k4, k4 from cn.
8-st LC Sl 4 sts to cn and hold to *front,* k4, k4 from cn.

K1, P1 RIB
(over an odd number of sts)
Row 1 (RS) K1, *p1, k1; rep from * to end.
Row 2 P1, *k1, p1; rep from * to end.
Rep rows 1 and 2 for k1, p1 rib.

NOTE
Selvage sts are included in the stitch counts but not in the finished measurements.

LEFT FRONT
With larger needles, cast on 7 sts.

Beg Chart 1
Row 1 (RS) Work 7 sts of chart 1. Cont to foll chart through row 21, end with a RS row. Cut yarn. Leave 21 sts on spare needle.
Cast-on row With larger needles, cast on 12 sts, place marker (pm), work chart row 22 over 21 sts on spare needle, pm, cast on 13 (17, 23) sts—46 (50, 56) sts.
Next row (RS) K1, [p1, k1] 6 (8, 11) times, sl marker, work row 23 over next 21 sts, sl marker, [k1, p1] 5 times, k2.
Next row Sl 1, p1, [k1, p1] 5 times, sl marker, work row 24 over next 21 sts, sl marker, p1, [k1, p1] 6 (8, 11) times. Keeping sts each side of markers in rib pats as established, work through row 30 of chart 1, end with a WS row.
Next row (RS) K to first marker, dec 0 (0, 1) st at beg of row, sl marker, work row 31 over next 21 sts, sl marker, k5, p1, [k1, p1] twice, k2—46 (50, 55) sts.
Next row Sl 1, [p1, k1] 3 times, p5, sl marker, work

STITCH KEY

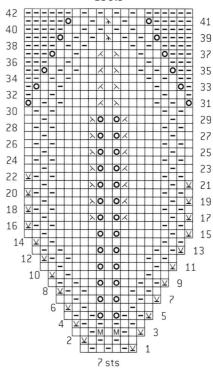

☐ k on RS, p on WS	☑ slip 1 wyib
⊟ p on RS, k on WS	5-st RPC
⊠ k2tog	5-st LPC
⊠ ssk	6-st RPC
○ yo	6-st LPC
⊼ SK2P	8-st RC
Ⓜ M1	8-st LC

CHART 1
21 sts

7 sts

row 32 over next 21 sts, sl marker, p to end. Keeping sts before first marker in St st and 12 sts after 2nd marker in rib pat as established, cont to foll chart 1 through row 42, end with a WS row.

Beg Chart 2

Row 43 (RS) K to first marker, sl marker, work chart row 43 over next 21 sts, sl marker, k5, p1, [k1, p1] twice, k2. Cont to foll chart 2 through row 48, end with a WS row.

Shape Side

Next (dec) row (RS) K2, ssk, work to end. Rep dec row every 14th row 3 times more. Work even on 42 (46, 51) sts through row 108, end with a WS row.

CHART 2

CHART 4

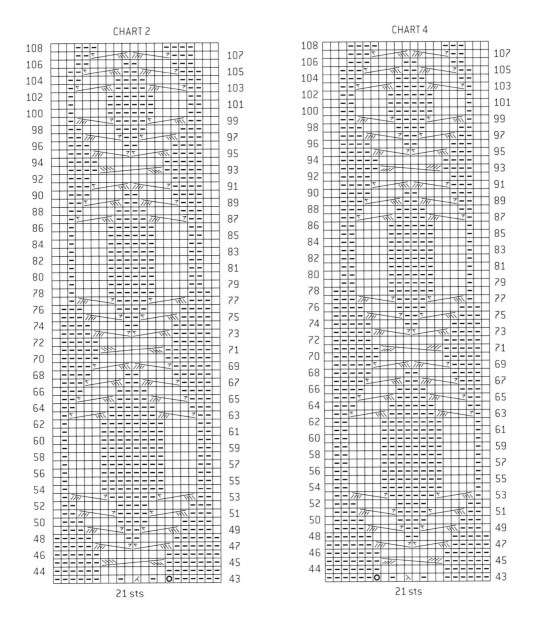

21 sts

21 sts

STITCH KEY

☐ k on RS, p on WS

⊟ p on RS, k on WS

k2tog

ssk

⊙ yo

SK2P

Ⓜ M1

slip 1 wyib

5-st RPC

5-st LPC

6-st RPC

6-st LPC

8-st RC

8-st LC

CHART 3

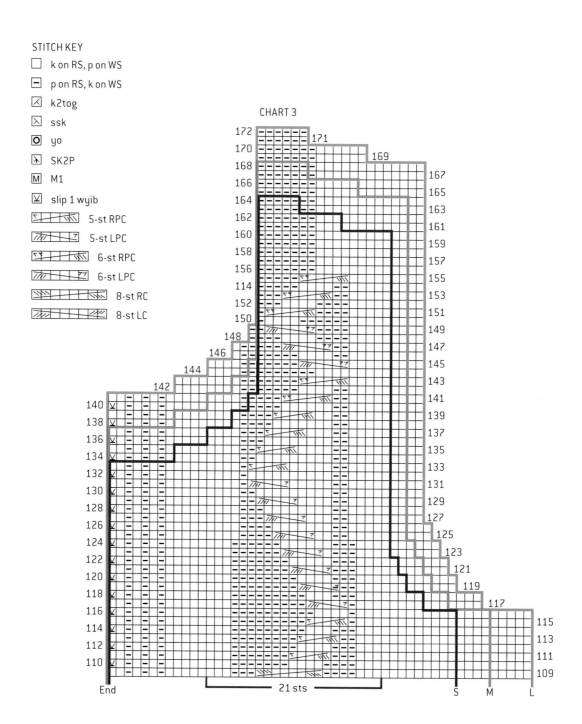

End

21 sts

S   M   L

CHART 5

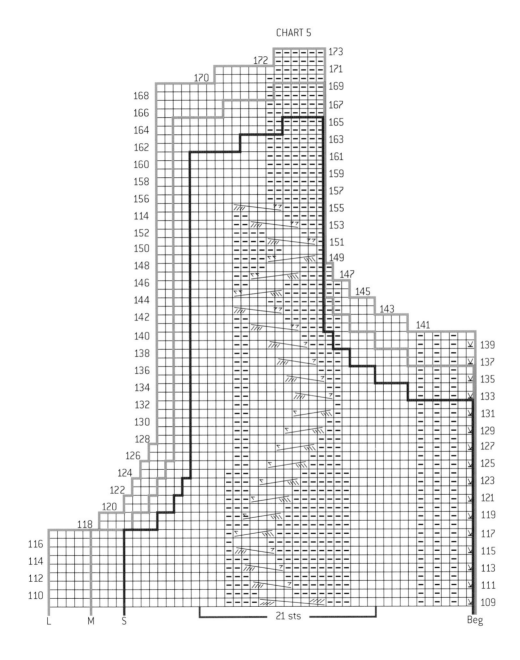

Beg Chart 3
Row 109 (RS) Beg and end chart 3 where indicated for size being made. Work even through row 116, end with a WS row. Piece should measure 15½"/39.5cm from beg.

Shape Armhole
Row 117 (RS) Bind off first 4 (5, 6) sts. At same (armhole) edge, bind off 2 (2, 3) sts once, then 1 st 2 (3, 4) times. Work even on 34 (36, 38) sts through row 133 (137, 141), end with a RS row.

Shape Neck
Row 134 (138, 142) (WS) Bind off first 8 sts. At same (neck) edge, bind off 4 sts once, 3 sts once, 2 sts once, then 1 st once. Work even on 16 (18, 20) sts through row 160 (164, 168), end with a WS row. Armhole should measure 7½ (8, 8½)"/19 (20.5, 21.5)cm.

Shape Shoulder
Row 161 (165, 169) (RS) Bind off first 6 (6, 7) sts. At same (armhole) edge, bind off 5 (6, 7) sts once, then 5 (6, 6) sts once.

RIGHT FRONT
Work as for left front to cast-on row.
Cast-on row With larger needles, cast on 13 (17, 23) sts, pm, work chart row 22 over 21 sts on spare needle, pm, cast on 12 sts—46 (50, 56) sts.
Next row (RS) Sl 1, k1, [p1, k1] 5 times, sl marker, work row 23 over next 21 sts, sl marker, k1 [p1, k1] 6 (8, 11) times.
Next row P1, [k1, p1] 6 (8, 11) times, sl marker, work row 24 over next 21 sts, sl marker, [p1, k1] 5 times, p2. Keeping sts each side of markers in rib pats as established, work through row 30 of chart, end with a WS row.
Next row (RS) Sl 1, [k1, p1] 3 times, k5, sl marker, work row 31 over next 21 sts, sl marker, k to end, dec 0 (0, 1) st at end of row—46 (50, 55) sts.
Next row P to marker, sl marker, work row 32 over next

21 sts, sl marker, p5, k1, [p1, k1] twice, p2. Keeping 12 sts before first marker in rib pat as established and sts after 2nd marker in St st, cont to foll chart through row 42, end with a WS row.

Beg Chart 4
Row 43 (RS) Sl 1, [k1, p1] 3 times, k5, sl marker, work chart row 43 over next 21 sts, sl marker, k to end. Cont to foll chart 4 through row 48, end with a WS row.

Shape Side
Next (dec) row (RS) Work to last 4 sts, k2tog, k2. Rep dec row every 14th row 3 times more. Work even on 42 (46, 51) sts through row 108, end with a WS row.

Beg Chart 5
Row 109 (RS) Beg and end chart 5 where indicated for size being made. Work even through row 117, end with a RS row.

Shape Armhole
Row 118 (WS) Bind off first 4 (5, 6) sts. At same (armhole) edge, bind off 2 (2, 3) sts once, then 1 st 2 (3, 4) times. Work even on 34 (36, 38) sts through row 132 (136, 140), end with a WS row.

Shape Neck
Row 133 (137, 141) (RS) Bind off first 8 sts. At same (neck) edge, bind off 4 sts once, 3 sts once, 2 sts once, then 1 st once. Work even on 16 (18, 20) sts through row 161 (165, 169), end with a RS row.

Shape Shoulder
Row 162 (166, 170) (WS) Bind off first 6 (6, 7) sts. At same (armhole) edge, bind off 5 (6, 7) sts once, then 5 (6, 6) sts once.

BACK
With larger needles, cast on 89 (99, 109) sts. Work in k1, p1 rib for 8 rows, end with a WS row. Cont in St st and work even for 20 rows, end with a WS row.

Shape Sides

Next (dec) row (RS) K2, ssk, k to last 4 sts, k2 tog, k2. Rep dec row every 14th row 3 times more. Work even on 81 (89, 99) sts until piece measures same length as left front to underarm, end with a WS row.

Shape Armholes

Bind off 4 (5, 6) sts at beg of next 2 rows, 2 (2, 3) sts at beg of next 2 rows, then 1 st at beg of next 4 (6, 8) rows. Work even on 65 (69, 73) sts until piece measures same length as left front to shoulder, end with a WS row. Place markers to mark center 27 sts on last WS row.

Shape Neck and Shoulders

Bind off 6 (6, 7) sts at beg of next 2 rows, 5 (6, 7) sts at beg of next 2 rows, then 5 (6, 6) sts at beg of next 2 rows. AT THE SAME TIME, join a 2nd ball of yarn and bind off center 27 sts. Working both sides at once, bind off 3 sts from each neck edge once.

FINISHING

Block pieces to measurements. Sew shoulder seams.

Neckband

With RS facing and smaller needles, pick up and k 34 sts evenly spaced along right front neck edge to shoulder seam, 41 sts along back neck edge to shoulder seam, then 34 sts along left front neck edge—109 sts.
Row 1 (WS) Sl 1, *p1, k1; rep from * to last 2 sts, end p2.
Row 2 Sl 1, *k1, p1; rep from * to last 2 sts, end k2. Rep rows 1 and 2 four times more. Bind off in rib.

Armbands

With RS facing and smaller needles, pick up and k 75 (81, 89) sts evenly spaced along armhole edge. Beg with row 2 (WS), work in k1, p1 rib for 5 rows. Bind off loosely in rib. Sew side and armband seams. On WS, sew one hook-and-eye set just above beg of neckband and rem set just below top edge of neckband. Ω

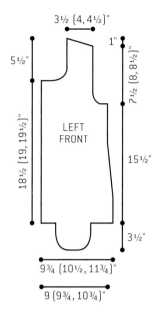

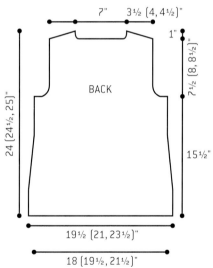

Winning Colors

This single-button tunic with rustic Fair Isle motifs and braided trim,
designed by **Marin Melchior**, is tailor-made for sitting by the fire at a cozy lodge.

SIZES
Sized for Small/Medium, Large/X-Large. Shown in size Large/X-Large.

FINISHED MEASUREMENTS
Bust 39 (42)"/99 (106.5)cm
Length 27½ (28)"/69.5 (71)cm

MATERIALS
220 Superwash Aran by Cascade Yarns, 3½oz/100g hanks, each approx 150yd/137.5m (superwash merino wool)
- 3 hanks each in #893 ruby (MC) and #854 navy (C)
- 2 hanks in #817 aran (A)
- 1 hank each in #1987 magenta (B), #845 denim (D), and #809 really red (E)
- Size 9 (5.5mm) circular needle, 36"/92cm long, *or size to obtain gauge*
- Spare size 9 (5.5mm) needle for 3-needle bind-off
- Two 1¼"/32mm buttons
- Two ⅞"/22mm buttons
- One heavy-weight black hair elastic (for button loop)
- Stitch markers
- Stitch holder

GAUGE
20 sts and 20 rows to 4"/10cm over chart pats using size 9 (5.5mm) needle. *Take time to check gauge.*

SHORT ROW WRAP & TURN (W&T)
On RS row (on WS row)
1) Wyib (wyif), sl next st purlwise.
2) Move yarn between the needles to the front (back).
3) Sl the same st back to LH needle. Turn work. One st is wrapped.
4) When working the wrapped st, insert RH needle under the wrap and work it tog with the corresponding st on needle to close wrap.

3-NEEDLE BIND-OFF
1) Hold right sides of pieces together on 2 needles. Insert 3rd needle knitwise into first st of each needle, and wrap yarn knitwise.
2) Knit these 2 sts together, and slip them off the needles. *Knit the next 2 sts together in the same manner.
3) Slip first st on 3rd needle over 2nd st and off needle. Rep from * in step 2 across row until all sts are bound off.

NOTE
Color charts are worked using the Fair Isle technique. Hold the color not in use loosely across the back of work and pull up from under the last color loosely to avoid holes in the work.

BACK
With MC, cast on 98 (106) sts.

*Begin Chart 1
Row 1 (RS) K1 (selvage st), work 8-st rep of row 1 of

Begin Chart 3

Row 1 (RS) K1 (selvage st), work the 12-st rep of row 1 of chart 3 a total of 8 times, then work the first 8 sts of chart 0 (1) times more, end k1 (selvage st). Cont to foll chart 3 in this way through row 19. Then, with MC, work 3 rows in St st.

Begin Chart 4

Row 1 (RS) K1 (selvage st), work 4-st rep of row 1 of chart 4 a total of 24 (26) times, k1 (selvage st). Cont to foll chart 4 in this way through row 7. Then, with MC, work 3 rows in St st.

Rep from * (66 rows) for color pat, AT THE SAME TIME, when piece measures 20"/51cm from beg, shape armhole.

Shape Armhole

Bind off 5 sts at beg of next 2 rows—88 (96) sts. Work even until armhole measures 7 (7½)"/18 (19) cm. Place sts on a st holder.

LEFT FRONT

With MC, cast on 51 (55) sts. Work in 66-row rep color pat as for back as foll:

For chart 1 Work 8-st rep 6 times, then rep first 2 (7) sts of chart once more.

For charts 2 and 4 Work 4-st rep 12 (13) times, then rep first 2 (3) sts of chart once more.

For chart 3 Work 12-st rep 4 times, then rep first 2 (7) sts of chart once more.

Work in this way until piece measures 20"/51cm from beg.

Shape Armhole and Neck

Next row (RS) Bind off 5 sts, work to last 6 sts, k2tog (neck dec), k4.

Rep neck dec every RS row 16 (15) times more, then every 4th row 0 (1) times—29 (33) sts. Work even, if necessary, until armhole measures same as back. Using 3-needle bind-off, join shoulders tog from the WS.

chart 1 a total of 12 (13) times, k1 (selvage st). Cont to foll chart 1 in this way through row 21. Then, with MC, work 3 rows in St st.

Begin Chart 2

Row 1 (RS) K1 (selvage st), work 4-st rep of row 1 of chart 2 a total of 24 (26) times, k1 (selvage st). Cont to foll chart 2 in this way through row 7. Then, with MC, work 3 rows in St st.

RIGHT FRONT

Work as for left front, reversing shaping, and work the neck dec row as k4, ssk, k to end of row.

FINISHING

Leaving last 7"/18cm of all 3 pieces free (for side vents), sew side seams tog.

Collar

From RS, with MC, beg at first neck shaping row of right front, pick up and k 40 (42) sts along right front neck edge, pm, pick up and k 30 sts along back neck edge, pm, pick up and k 40 (42) sts along left front neck edge—110 (114) sts. Purl 1 row, knit 1 row. Now, working from WS of collar (while RS of garment is facing you), work as foll:
Inc row 1 (RS of collar) *K to 1 st before marker, M1R, sl marker, M1L; rep from * once, k to end.
Row 2 Purl.
Rep inc row 1 every RS row 7 times more, AT THE SAME TIME, beg working short row shaping as foll:
Short row 1 (RS) Knit to last 5 sts, w&t.
Short row 2 Purl to last 5 sts, w&t.
Short row 3 Knit to 4 sts before previous wrapped st, w&t.

Short row 4 Purl to 4 sts before previous wrapped st, w&t.
Short row 5 Knit to 3 sts before previous wrapped st, w&t.
Short row 6 Purl to 3 sts before previous wrapped st, w&t.
Rep short rows 5 and 6 four times more—142 (146) sts. K to end of next row, closing wraps, p to end of next row, closing wraps. Then, beg and end with k1 (selvage st), work chart 4 pat for 7 rows. Work 2 rows in St st with MC.

Latvian Plait Trim

Set-up row 1 (WS) *P1 with A, p1 with MC; rep from * to end.
Row 2 (RS) *Wyif, p1 with MC, p1 with A, always carrying yarn in front of work and crossing new color over color just used; rep from * to end.
Row 3 *Wyib, k1 with A, k1 with MC, always carrying yarn in back and crossing new color undercolor just used; rep from * to end.
With C, work in St st for 4 rows for hem. Do *not* bind off. Fold hem to WS and sew loops from needle to WS until all sts are joined.

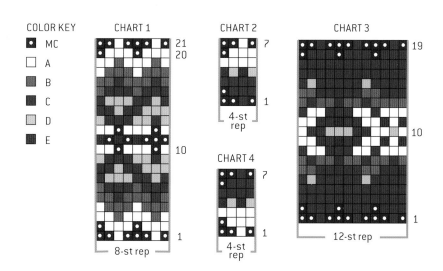

Back Hem Edging

With A, pick up and k 36 sts along side vent edge, 98 (106) sts along lower back edge, and 36 sts along side vent edge. Work Latvian plait trim for 3 rows (as on collar), then work 6 rows in St st with C (for hem). Sew hem in place st by st as on collar.

Right Front Hem Edging

With A, pick up and k 35 sts along side vent edge, 51 (55) sts along lower edge, and 98 (100) sts along center front edge. Complete as for back hem edging. Work left front hem edging in same way.

Armhole Trims

Work as for other hem edgings on 78 (84) sts only, work in rnds with first set-up rnd in knit and other 2 rnds in purl. For button closure, first stretch hair elastic and knot securely at center. Using photo as guide, sew one large button at outside of left front, securing with one smaller button to anchor in back. Work right front button in same way. Secure elastic in place on one side, then use free end of elastic to button in place. ♎

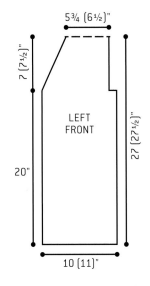

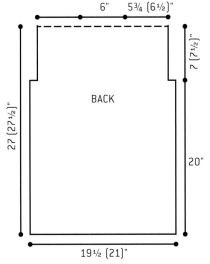

Terlingua

James Emslie brings subtle beauty to a casual rolled-edge vest with pretty gathers at the shoulders and arrow-shaped motifs on the back and fronts.

SIZES
Sized for Small/Medium, Large/1X, 2X. Shown in size Small/Medium.

FINISHED MEASUREMENTS
Bust 43 (50, 54)"/109 (127, 137)cm
Length 22 (22½, 23)"/56 (57, 58.5)cm
Note Bust measurements are given with fronts meeting; note that vest is loose-fitting to allow fronts to roll.

MATERIALS
220 Superwash Aran by Cascade Yarns, 3½oz/100g hanks, each approx 150yd/137.5m (superwash merino wool)
- 4 (5, 5) hanks in #1958 sapphire
- One pair size 8 (5mm) needles *or size to obtain gauge*
- Stitch markers in different colors
- Stitch holders

GAUGE
16 sts and 22 rows to 4"/10cm over St st using size 8 (5mm) needles. *Take time to check gauge.*

STITCH GLOSSARY
3-st gather P3tog, do not drop sts from LH needle, yo, p3tog the same 3 sts once more, letting sts drop from LH needle.

BACK
Cast on 86 (100, 108) sts. Knit 2 rows.
Next row (RS) K1, *yo, k2tog; rep from * to last st, k1.
Next row (WS) Knit.
Work in St st (k on RS, p on WS) until piece measures 13 (13½, 14)"/33 (34.5, 35.5)cm from beg, end with a WS row.

Shape Armhole
Note Read before cont to knit.
Bind off 2 (4, 4) sts at beg of next 2 rows.
Dec 1 st each side of next row, then every other row 0 (2, 3) times, then every 4th row 10 times, AT THE SAME TIME, after 4 rows of armhole shaping have been worked, mark center 4 sts and work displacement pat as foll:
Displacement row 1 (RS) K to 3 sts before marker, place new marker, 3-st gather, remove marker, k to

next marker, remove marker, 3-st gather, place new marker, k to end.

Cont armhole shaping, repeat displacement row 1 every 4th row 8 times more, AT THE SAME TIME, after 4 displacement rows have been worked, work 3 rows even, then place different-color markers to mark center 2 sts on last row (center markers) and work center back neck shaping as foll:

Note Cont to work displacement of the 3-st gathers and armhole shaping while shaping center back neck.

Displacement row 2 (RS) Work to center marker, sl marker, M1R, k to next center marker, M1L, sl marker, work to end. Work 1 row even.

Displacement row 3 (RS) Work to center marker, sl marker, M1R, p1, k to 1 st before next center marker, p1, M1L, sl marker, work to end.

Rep displacement row 3 every other row 12 times more—30 sts between center markers, 29 (32, 35) sts each side after all shaping is complete. Work 1 WS row.

Next row (RS) K6, [p3tog] 6 (7, 8) times, k5, bind off center 30 sts, k5, [p3tog] 6 (7, 8) times, k6.

Place rem 17 (18, 19) sts each side on st holders for shoulders.

LEFT FRONT

Cast on 42 (50, 56) sts. Knit 2 rows.

Next row (RS) K1, *yo, k2tog; rep from * to last st, k1.
Next row (WS) Knit, dec 0 (1, 0) sts—42 (49, 56) sts.
Work in St st (k on RS, p on WS) until piece measures same as back to armhole, end with a WS row.

Shape Armhole

Note Read before cont to knit.

Shape armhole at side edge (beg of RS rows) as for back, AT THE SAME TIME, when 4 rows of armhole shaping have been worked, place marker 2 sts from front edge and work displacement pat as foll:

Displacement row 1 (RS) K to 3 sts before marker, place new marker, 3-st gather, remove marker, k to end.

Cont armhole shaping, repeat displacement row 1 every 4th row 8 times more. Work even until armhole measures same as back to shoulder, end with a WS row—29 (32, 36) sts when shaping is complete.

Next row (RS) K6, [p3tog] 6 (7, 8) times, k5.
Place rem 17 (18, 19) sts on st holder.

RIGHT FRONT

Work as for left front, reversing all shaping and displacement of 3-st gathers.

FINISHING

Graft shoulder seams. Sew side seams. Ω

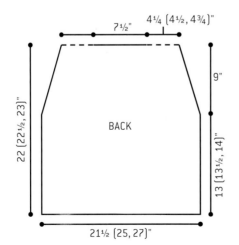

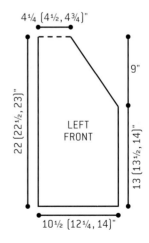

Sky Beauty

Theresa Schabes flatters the figure with blocks of color
set off by stripes that curve in all the right places.

SIZES
Sized for Small, Medium, Large, 1X, 2X, 3X. Shown in
size Small.

FINISHED MEASUREMENTS
Bust 34 (38, 42, 46, 50, 54)"/86.5 (96.5, 106.5, 117,
127, 137)cm
Length 19½ (20, 21, 21½, 22½, 23)"/49.5 (51, 53.5,
54.5, 57, 58.5)cm

MATERIALS
220 Superwash Aran by Cascade Yarns, 3½oz/100g
hanks, each approx 150yd/137.5m (superwash
merino wool)
- 2 (3, 3, 3, 4, 4) hanks in #845 denim (C)
- 1 hank each in #854 navy (A) and #1992 deep
  jungle (B)
- One pair each sizes 6 and 8 (4 and 5mm) needles
  or size to obtain gauge
- Size 6 (4mm) circular needle, 16"/40cm long
- Stitch holder
- Stitch marker
- Bobbins

GAUGE
17 sts and 24 rows to 4"/10cm over St st using
larger needles. *Take time to check gauge.*

NOTES
1) When changing color, pick up new color from
under dropped color to prevent holes.
2) Use a separate ball or bobbin of yarn for each
color section.
3) Piece is worked with a St st selvage stitch,
which is included in the stitch counts but not
in the schematic measurements.

K1, P1 RIB
(over an odd number of sts)
Row 1 (RS) K1, *p1, k1; rep from * to end.
Row 2 P1, *k1, p1; rep from * to end.
Rep rows 1 and 2 for k1, p1 rib.

BACK
With smaller needles and A, cast on 75 (83, 91, 101,
109, 117) sts. Work in k1, p1 rib for 6 (6, 6, 8, 8, 8)
rows, dec 1 st at end of last row and end with a WS
row—74 (82, 90, 100, 108, 116) sts.
Change to larger needles and St st (k on RS, p on WS).

Beg Hourglass Pat
Next row (RS) With B, k6 (8, 10, 12, 14, 16); with A,
k3 (3, 3, 4, 4, 4); with C, k56 (60, 64, 68, 72, 76); with
A, k3 (3, 3, 4, 4, 4); with B, k6 (8, 10, 12, 14, 16).
Next row With B, p6 (8, 10, 12, 14, 16); with A, p3
(3, 3, 4, 4, 4); with C, p56 (60, 64, 68, 72, 76); with A,
p3 (3, 3, 4, 4, 4); with B, p6 (8, 10, 12, 14, 16).
Rep last 2 rows 3 times more.

Advance Pat Toward Center
Advance row 1 (RS) With B, k to last B st, M1, k1; with A, k3 (3, 3, 4, 4, 4); with C, ssk, k to last 2 C sts, k2tog; with A, k3 (3, 3, 4, 4, 4); with B, k1, M1, k to end. Work even as established for 7 rows, end with a WS row. Rep advance row 1. Work even as established for 5 rows, end with a WS row. *Rep advance row 1. Work even as established for 3 rows, end with a WS row; rep from * once more.

Shape Waist
Next (dec) row (RS) With B, k to end of B sts; with A, k3 (3, 3, 4, 4, 4); with C, ssk, k to last 2 C sts, k2tog; with A, k3 (3, 3, 4, 4, 4); with B, k to end. Rep dec row every 4th row twice more—68 (76, 84, 94, 102, 110) sts. Work 7 rows more as established after last dec row, end with a WS row.
Next (inc) row (RS) With B, k to end of B sts; with A, k3 (3, 3, 4, 4, 4); with MC, k1, M1, k to last st, M1, k1; with A, k3 (3, 3, 4, 4, 4); with B, k to end. Rep inc row every 4th row twice more—74 (82, 90, 100, 108, 116) sts. Work 3 rows more after last inc row, end with a WS row.

Advance Pat Toward Sides
Advance row 2 (RS) With B, k to last 2 sts, k2tog; with A, k3 (3, 3, 4, 4, 4); with C, k1, M1, k to last C st, M1, k1; with A, k3 (3, 3, 4, 4, 4); with B, ssk, k to end. Rep advance row 2 every other row 3 times more. Work even (if necessary) until piece measures 12 (12, 12½, 12½, 13, 13)"/30.5 (30.5, 31.5, 31.5, 33, 33)cm from beg, end with a WS row.

Shape Armholes
Bind off 5 (6, 7, 8, 9, 9) sts at beg of next 2 rows, 2 (2, 2, 3, 3, 3) sts at beg of next 2 rows, then 2 (2, 2, 2, 2, 3) sts at beg of next 2 rows. Dec 1 st each side on next row, then every other row 2 (3, 4, 5, 6) times more. Work even on 50 (56, 60, 64, 68, 72) sts until armhole measures 6 (6½, 7, 7½, 8, 8½)"/15 (16.5, 17.5, 19, 20.5, 21.5)cm, end with a WS row.

Shape Neck
Next row (RS) K19 (22, 23, 25, 26, 28), join a 2nd ball of yarn and bind off center 12 (12, 14, 14, 16, 16) sts, k to end. Working both sides at once, bind off 5 sts from each neck edge once, 2 sts once, then 1 st twice—10 (13, 14, 16, 17, 19) sts each side. AT THE SAME TIME, when armhole measures 7½ (8, 8½, 9, 9½, 10)"/19 (20.5, 21.5, 23, 24, 25.5)cm, end with a WS row.

Shape Shoulders
Bind off 5 (7, 7, 8, 9, 10) sts at beg of next 2 rows, then 5 (6, 7, 8, 8, 9) sts at beg of next 2 rows.

FRONT
Work as for back until armhole measures 2½ (3, 3½, 4, 4½, 5)"/6 (7.5, 9, 10, 11.5, 12.5)cm, end with a WS row.

Shape Neck
Next row (RS) K22 (25, 26, 28, 29, 31), sl center 6 (6, 8, 8, 10, 10) sts to a st holder, join a 2nd ball of yarn, k to end. Working both sides at once, bind off 2 sts from each neck edge twice, end with a WS row.
Next (dec) row (RS) With first ball of yarn, k to last 3 sts, k2tog, k1; with 2nd ball of yarn, k1, ssk, k to end. Purl next row. Rep last 2 rows 7 times more. Work even on 10 (13, 14, 16, 17, 19) sts each side until piece measures same length as back to shoulder, end with a WS row. Shape shoulders as for back.

FINISHING
Block pieces to measurements. Sew shoulder and side seams.

Neckband
With RS facing, circular needle, and A, pick up and k 32 sts along left front neck edge, k6 (6, 8, 8, 10, 10) from holder, pick up and k 32 sts along right neck edge to shoulder seam, pick up and k 34 (34, 36, 36, 38, 38) sts along back neck edge—104 (104, 108, 108,

112, 112) sts. Pm for beg of rnds. Work around in k1, p1 rib for 5 (5, 5, 6, 6, 6) rnds. Bind off loosely in rib.

Armbands

With RS facing, circular needle and A, pick up and k 88 (94, 100, 106, 110, 116) sts evenly spaced around armhole edge. Pm for beg of rnds. Work around in k1, p1 rib for 5 (5, 5, 6, 6, 6) rnds. Bind off loosely in rib. Ω

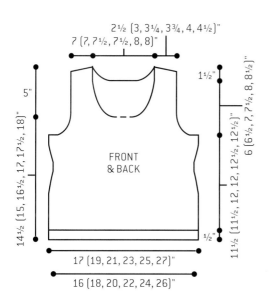

2½ (3, 3¼, 3¾, 4, 4½)"

7 (7, 7½, 7½, 8, 8)"

1½"

5"

6 (6½, 7, 7½, 8, 8½)"

14½ (15, 16½, 17, 17½, 18)"

11½ (11½, 12, 12, 12½, 12½)"

FRONT & BACK

½"

17 (19, 21, 23, 25, 27)"

16 (18, 20, 22, 24, 26)"

Meadow Star

Sandi Prosser gracefully combines disparate design elements: a welted lower band, a moss stitch torso, and pretty leaf panels leading to the shoulders.

SIZES

Sized for Small, Medium, Large, X-Large, XX-Large. Shown in size Small.

FINISHED MEASUREMENTS

Bust 36 (40, 43½, 49, 52½)"/91.5 (101.5, 110.5, 124.5, 133.5)cm

Length 26½ (27, 27½, 28, 28)"/67.5 (68.5, 70, 71, 71)cm

MATERIALS

220 Superwash Aran by Cascade Yarns, 3½oz/100g hanks, each approx 150yd/137.5m (superwash merino wool)

- 6 (7, 8, 9, 9) hanks in #1995 cactus
- One pair each sizes 8 and 9 (5 and 5.5mm) needles *or size to obtain gauge*
- Size 8 (5mm) circular needle, 24"/60cm long
- Stitch holder
- Stitch marker

GAUGES

18 sts and 25 rows to 4"/10cm over St st using smaller needles.

18 sts and 28 rows to 4"/10cm over moss st using larger needles.

Take time to check gauges.

MOSS STITCH

(multiple of 4 sts plus 2)

Row 1 (RS) *K2, p2; rep from * to last 2 sts, k2.

Rows 2 and 3 P2, *k2, p2; rep from * to end.

Row 4 *K2, p2; rep from * to last 2 sts, k2.

Rep rows 1–4 for moss stitch.

LEAF PANEL

(worked over 26 sts, inc to 30 sts, dec to 26 sts)

Row 1 (WS) K5, p5, k4, p3, k9.

Row 2 P7, p2tog, kfb, k2, p4, k2, yo, k1, yo, k2, p5—28 sts.

Row 3 K5, p7, k4, p2, k1, p1, k8.

Row 4 P6, p2tog, k1, pfb, k2, p4, k3, yo, k1, yo, k3, p5—30 sts.

Row 5 K5, p9, k4, p2, k2, p1, k7.

Row 6 P5, p2tog, k1, pfb, p1, k2, p4, ssk, k5, k2tog, p5—28 sts.

Row 7 K5, p7, k4, p2, k3, p1, k6.

Row 8 P4, p2tog, k1, pfb, p2, k2, p4, ssk, k3, k2tog, p5—26 sts.

Row 9 K5, p5, k4, p2, k4, p1, k5.

Row 10 P5, yo, k1, yo, p4, k2, p4, ssk, k1, k2tog, p5.

Row 11 K5, p3, k4, p2, k4, p3, k5.

Row 12 P5, [yo, k1] twice, k1, p4, k1, M1, k1, p2tog, p2, S2KP, p5.

Row 13 K9, p3, k4, p5, k5.

Row 14 P5, k2, yo, k1, yo, k2, p4, k1, kfb, k1, p2tog, p7—28 sts.

Row 15 K8, p1, k1, p2, k4, p7, k5.

Row 21 K5, p1, k4, p2, k4, p5, k5.

Row 22 P5, ssk, k1, k2tog, p4, k2, p4, yo, k1, yo, p5.

Row 23 K5, p3, k4, p2, k4, p3, k5.

Row 24 P5, S2KP, p2, p2tog, k1, M1, k1, p4, [yo, k1] twice, k1, p5.

Rep rows 1–24 for leaf panel.

WELT PATTERN

Rows 1 and 3 (RS) Sl 1 purlwise wyif, purl to end of row.

Rows 2 and 4 Knit.

Rows 5 and 7 Sl 1 purlwise wyif, knit to end of row.

Rows 6 and 8 Purl.

Rep rows 1–8 for welt pattern.

NOTES

1) Lower band of front and back are worked horizontally from side seam to side seam.

2) Increased stitches in leaf panel are not included in stitch counts.

BACK

Lower Band

With smaller needles, cast on 17 sts. Beg with row 1, rep rows 1–8 of welt pat 20 (22, 24, 27, 29) times, then rows 1–4 once. Bind off first 16 sts, leaving last st on RH needle. Turn work 90 degrees clockwise.

Main Body

With RS facing, pick up and k 81 (89, 97, 109, 117) sts along top edge of lower band—82 (90, 98, 110, 118) sts.

Next row (WS) Knit.

Change to larger needles. Beg with row 1, work in moss st until piece measures 15"/38cm from beg, end with a WS row.

Change to smaller needles. Purl 4 rows.

Set-up row (RS) P17 (21, 24, 30, 33), M1 p-st, p7, M1 p-st, p17 (17, 18, 18, 19), M1, p17 (17, 18, 18, 19), M1 p-st, p7, M1 p-st, p17 (21, 24, 30, 33)—87 (95, 103, 115, 123) sts.

Row 16 P5, k3, yo, k1, yo, k3, p4, k2, pfb, k1, p2tog, p6—30 sts.

Row 17 K7, p1, k2, p2, k4, p9, k5.

Row 18 P5, ssk, k5, k2tog, p4, k2, p1, pfb, k1, p2tog, p5—28 sts.

Row 19 K6, p1, k3, p2, k4, p7, k5.

Row 20 P5, ssk, k3, k2tog, p4, k2, p2, pfb, k1, p2tog, p4—26 sts.

Next row (WS) K7 (11, 14, 20, 23), work row 13 of leaf panel over next 26 sts, k21 (21, 23, 23, 25), work row 1 of leaf panel over next 26 sts, k7 (11, 14, 20, 23).

Next row (RS) P7 (11, 14, 20, 23), work row 2 of leaf panel over next 26 sts, p21 (21, 23, 23, 25), work row 14 of leaf panel over next 26 sts, p7 (11, 14, 20, 23). Cont in this manner until row 24 of leaf panel is complete. Rep rows 1–24 of leaf panel until piece measures 18½"/47cm from beg, end with a WS row.

Shape Armhole
Cont in pat as established, bind off 5 (5, 6, 7, 8) sts at beg of next 2 rows. Dec 1 st at each end of next RS row, then every other row 3 (4, 4, 5, 7) times more— 69 (75, 81, 89, 93) sts. Work even in pat until armhole measures 8 (8½, 9, 9½, 9½)"/20 (21.5, 23, 24, 24) cm, end with a WS row.

Next row (RS) Bind off 21 (24, 26, 30, 31) sts, p27 (27, 29, 29, 31), bind off rem 21 (24, 26, 30, 31) sts. Place 27 (27, 29, 29, 31) sts on holder for back neck.

FRONT
Work as for back until piece measures 17"/43cm from beg, end with a WS row. Mark center st.

Shape Neck
Next row (RS) Work to center marked st and place this st on a st holder, join a 2nd ball of yarn and work in pat to end of row. Working both sides at once, dec 1 st at each neck edge on next RS row, then every 4th row 12 (12, 13, 13, 14) times more. AT THE SAME TIME, when piece measures 18½"/47cm from beg, shape armholes as for back—21 (24, 26, 30, 31) sts rem each side for shoulder after all shaping is complete. Work even in pat until armhole measures 8 (8½, 9, 9½, 9½)"/20 (21.5, 23, 24, 24)cm, end with a WS row. Bind off rem 21 (24, 26, 30, 31) sts each side for shoulder.

FINISHING
Block pieces to measurements. Sew shoulder seams.

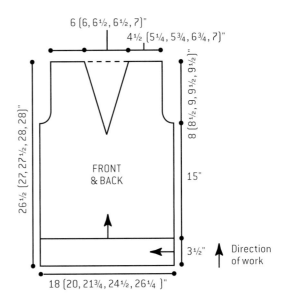

6 (6, 6½, 6½, 7)"
4½ (5¼, 5¾, 6¾, 7)"
8 (8½, 9, 9½, 9½)"
26½ (27, 27½, 28, 28)"

FRONT & BACK

15"

3½"
Direction of work

18 (20, 21¾, 24½, 26¼)"

Neck Edging
With circular needle and RS facing, beg at left shoulder seam, pick up and k 53 (55, 57, 59, 59) sts evenly along left front neck edge, place marker, k1 from front st holder, place marker, pick up and k 53 (55, 57, 59, 59) sts evenly along right front neck edge to shoulder, pick up and k 27 (27, 29, 29, 31) sts from back neck st holder—134 (138, 144, 148, 150) sts. Join and work in rnds.

Rnd 1 Purl to 2 sts before first marker, p2tog, slip marker (sm), p1, sm, p2tog tbl, purl to end of rnd.
Rnd 2 Knit.
Rep rnds 1–2 once more. Bind off all sts purlwise.

Armhole Edging
With smaller needles and RS facing, pick up and k 96 (102, 108, 114, 114) sts evenly around armhole opening. Knit 4 rows. Bind off all sts knitwise. Sew side and armhole edging seam. Ω

Beholder

Yoko Hatta takes a basic cable and makes a bold statement
by repeating it in wide panels down the front and back.

SIZES
Sized for X-Small, Small, Medium, Large, 1X, 2X. Shown
in size X-Small.

FINISHED MEASUREMENTS
Bust 32 (36, 40, 44, 48, 52)"/81 (91.5, 101.5,
111.5, 122, 132)cm
Length 24 (24, 24½, 24½, 25, 25)"/61 (61, 62,
62, 63.5, 63.5)cm

MATERIALS
220 Superwash Aran by Cascade Yarns, 3½oz/100g
hanks, each approx 150yd/137.5m (superwash
merino wool)
- 5 (5, 6, 6, 7, 8) 3½oz/100g hanks in #1946 silver grey
- One pair each sizes 7 and 9 (4.5 and 5.5mm)
  needles *or size to obtain gauge*
- Size 7 (4.5mm) circular needle, 16"/40cm long
- Cable needle (cn)
- Stitch markers
- Stitch holders

GAUGE
16 sts and 24 rows to 4"/10cm over St st using larger
needles. *Take time to check gauge.*

3-NEEDLE BIND-OFF
1) Hold right sides of pieces together on 2 needles.
Insert 3rd needle knitwise into first st of each needle,
and wrap yarn knitwise.

2) Knit these 2 sts together, and slip them off the
needles. *Knit the next 2 sts together in the same
manner.
3) Slip first st on 3rd needle over 2nd st and off
needle. Rep from * in step 2 across row until all sts are
bound off.

STITCH GLOSSARY
6-st LC Sl 3 sts to cn and hold to *front*, k3, k3
from cn.

NOTE
When shaping front neck, discontinue crossing cables.

BACK
With smaller needles, cast on 86 (94, 102, 110, 118,
126) sts.
Row 1 (RS) K2, *p2, k2; rep from * to end.
Row 2 (WS) P2, *k2, p2; rep from * to end.
Rep rows 1 and 2 for k2, p2 rib until piece measures
3¼"/8cm from beg, end with a WS row. Change to
larger needles.

Begin Chart
Row 1 (RS) K14 (18, 22, 26, 30, 34), place marker
(pm), work chart to rep line, work 16-st rep 3 times,
pm, k14 (18, 22, 26, 30, 34).
Row 2 (WS) Purl to marker, work 16-st rep 3 times,
work to end of chart, purl to end.
Cont to work chart in this way through row 12, then
rep rows 5–12, working sts outside of chart in St st,
until piece measures 15¼ (15¼, 15¼, 14¾, 15¼,

14¾)"/38.5 (38.5, 38.5, 37.5, 38.5, 37.5)cm from beg, end with a WS row.

Shape Armholes

Bind off 5 (5, 6, 6, 7, 7) sts at beg of next 2 rows, 3 (4, 4, 5, 5, 5) sts at beg of next 2 rows, 2 (3, 3, 3, 4, 4) sts at beg of next 2 rows. Dec 1 st each side of next row, then every other row 2 (2, 2, 3, 3, 5) times more, then every 4th row 1 (1, 2, 2, 2, 2) times—58 (62, 66, 70, 74, 78) sts.
Work even until armhole measures 8 (8, 8½, 9, 9, 9½)"/ 20.5 (20.5, 21.5, 23, 23, 24)cm, end with a WS row.

Shape Back Neck

Next row (RS) K13 (15, 17, 19, 21, 23), join 2nd ball of yarn and bind off center 32 sts, k to end.
Working both sides at once, bind off 2 sts from each

neck edge once, then 1 st once. Place rem 10 (12, 14, 16, 18, 20) sts each side on st holders.

FRONT

Work as for back until armhole shaping is complete, end with a WS row. Armhole measures approx 2¾ (2¾, 3¼, 3¾, 3¾, 4¼)"/7 (7, 8, 9.5, 9.5, 11)cm.

Shape Front Neck

Next row (RS) K24 (26, 28, 30, 32, 34), join 2nd ball of yarn and bind off center 10 sts, k to end.
Working both sides at once, bind off 4 sts from each neck edge once, 3 sts once, 2 sts once. Dec 1 st at each neck edge every other row 3 times, then every 4th row twice. Work even on rem 10 (12, 14, 16, 18, 20) sts until armhole measures same as back to shoulder, end with a WS row. Place sts each side on st holders.

FINISHING

Block pieces lightly to measurements. Join shoulders using 3-needle bind-off.

Neck Trim

With RS facing and circular needle, beg at left shoulder seam, pick up and k 34 sts along shaped left front neck edge, 6 sts along front neck, 34 sts along shaped right front neck edge, 34 sts along back neck edge—108 sts. Place marker for beg of rnd.
Rnd 1 *K2, p2; rep from * to end.
Rep rnd 1 for 5 rnds more. Bind off in pat.

Armhole Trim

With RS facing and circular needle, pick up and k 98 (98, 102, 110, 110, 114) sts evenly around armhole edge.
Row 1 (WS) P2, *k2, p2; rep from * to end.
Cont in k2, p2 rib as established for 5 rows more. Bind off in rib.
Sew side seams, including armhole trim seam. Ω

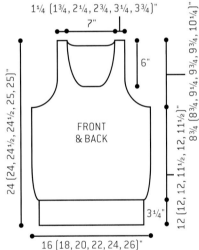

$1\frac{1}{4}$ ($1\frac{3}{4}$, $2\frac{1}{4}$, $2\frac{3}{4}$, $3\frac{1}{4}$, $3\frac{3}{4}$)"

7"

6"

$8\frac{3}{4}$ ($8\frac{3}{4}$, $9\frac{1}{4}$, $9\frac{3}{4}$, $9\frac{3}{4}$, $10\frac{1}{4}$)"

12 (12, 12, $11\frac{1}{2}$, 12, $11\frac{1}{2}$)"

24 (24, $24\frac{1}{2}$, $24\frac{1}{2}$, 25, 25)"

FRONT & BACK

$3\frac{1}{4}$"

16 (18, 20, 22, 24, 26)"

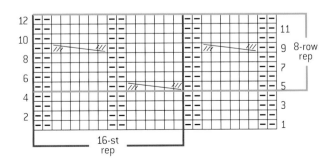

8-row rep

16-st rep

STITCH KEY

☐ k on RS, p on WS

⊟ p on RS, k on WS

6-st LC

Miss Woodford

This houndstooth-check design by **Tammy Eigeman Thompson** may be menswear-inspired, but it belongs in the wardrobe of every fashionable female.

SIZES
Sized for Small, Medium, Large. Shown in size Small.

FINISHED MEASUREMENTS
Bust (closed) 34 (37, 40)"/86.5 (94, 101.5)cm
Length 20 (20½, 21)"/51 (52, 53.5)cm

MATERIALS
220 Superwash Aran by Cascade Yarns, 3½ oz/100g hanks, each approx 150yd/137.5m (superwash merino wool)
- 3 (4, 4) hanks in #1994 dusky green (MC)
- 2 (3, 3) hanks in #875 feather grey (CC)
- Size 7 (4.5mm) circular needle, 32"/80cm long, *or size to obtain gauge*
- One each size 5 (3.75mm) circular needle, 16"/40cm and 32"/80cm long
- 3 size 5 (3.75mm) double-pointed needles (dpns) for pocket trim
- Spare size 7 (4.5mm) needle for 3-needle bind-off
- 5 buttons
- Stitch holders
- Stitch markers
- Scrap yarn

GAUGE
21 sts and 23 rows to 4"/10cm over chart pat using larger needle. *Take time to check gauge.*

3-NEEDLE BIND-OFF
1) Hold wrong sides of pieces together on 2 needles. Insert 3rd needle knitwise into first st of each needle, and wrap yarn knitwise.
2) Knit these 2 sts together, and slip them off the needles. *Knit the next 2 sts together in the same manner.
3) Slip first st on 3rd needle over 2nd st and off needle. Rep from * in step 2 across row until all sts are bound off.

K1, P1 RIB
(over an even number of sts)
Row 1 (RS) *K1, p1; rep from * to end.
Rep row 1 for k1, p1.

NOTE
Vest is worked in one piece to the armholes. Circular needle is used to accommodate large number of sts. Do not join.

BODY
With smaller 32"/80cm circular needle and MC, cast on 153 (166, 180) sts. Work in St st (k on RS, p on WS) for 6 rows.
Purl 2 rows for turning ridge. Work 4 rows in St st, inc 25 (28, 30) sts evenly across last row—178 (194, 210) sts.
Change to larger needle.

Begin Chart

Row 1 (RS) Sl 1, work 4-st rep of chart pat 11 (12, 13) times for right front, work 4-st rep of chart pat 22 (24, 26) times for back, work 4-st rep of chart pat 11 (12, 13) times for left front, k1 in MC.

Row 2 Sl 1, work 4-st rep of chart pat 11 (12, 13) times for right front, work 4-st rep of chart pat 22 (24, 26) times for back, work 4-st rep of chart pat 11 (12, 13) times for left front, p1 in MC.

Cont in this manner, rep rows 1–4 of chart pat until piece measures 5"/12.5cm from turning ridge, end with a WS row.

Place Pockets

Next row (RS) Cont in pat over next 12 sts, k20 with scrap yarn, slide these 20 sts back to LH needle and knit them again in pat, cont in pat to last 32 sts, k20 with scrap yarn, sl these 20 sts back to LH needle and work in pat to end of row.

Cont in pat until piece measures 12"/30.5cm from turning ridge, end with a WS row.

Right Front

Next row (RS) Sl 1, work next 38 (42, 44) sts in pat for right front, turn.

Next row (WS) Work in pat to end of row.

Shape Neck

Cont in pat on sts for right front *only* and dec 1 st for armhole at end of next 1 (1, 2) RS rows, AT THE SAME TIME, work neck decs at beg of RS rows as foll: Sl 1, k2tog tbl, work to end of row. Rep neck dec every 4th row 6 (5, 5) times more, then every other row 9 (12, 13) times. When all shaping is complete, work even on rem 21 (23, 24) sts until armhole measures 8 (8½, 9)"/20.5 (21.5, 23)cm, end with a WS row. Place sts on holder.

Back

Rejoin yarn to RS and bind off 14 (14, 16) sts, cont in pat until 74 (82, 88) back sts are on RH needle, turn.

Next row (WS) Work in pat to end of row.
Cont in pat over sts for back and dec 1 st each side of next 1 (1, 2) RS rows—72 (80, 84) sts rem for back. Work even until piece measures same as right front. Place 21 (23, 24) sts each side on holders for shoulders. Place center 30 (34, 36) sts on scrap yarn for back neck.

Left Front

Rejoin yarn to RS and bind off 14 (14, 16) sts. Work as for right front, reversing all shaping by working armhole decs at beg of RS rows and neck decs as k2tog, k1 at end of RS rows. Cont to sl first st of WS rows.

FINISHING

Join shoulders using 3-needle bind-off with WS tog.

Front and Neck Band

Place markers for 5 buttonholes along right front edge.
With RS facing, smaller 32"/80cm circular needle and MC, pick up and k 76 (78, 80) sts along right front edge, k 30 (34, 36) back neck sts from holder, pick up and k 76 (78, 80) sts along left front edge—182 (190, 196) sts.
Work in k1, p1 rib for 3 rows.
Next (buttonhole) row (RS) [Work in rib to marker, bind off 2 sts] 5 times, rib to end.
Next row Work in rib, casting on 2 sts over each buttonhole.
Work 3 rows more in rib. Bind off.

Armhole Trim

With smaller, 16"/40cm circular needle, pick up and k 82 (86, 90) sts around armhole, pm for beg of rnd. Work in k1, p1 rib for 4 rnds. Bind off.

Pocket

Carefully remove scrap yarn from pockets and place open sts on 2 dpns.

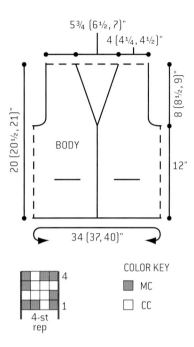

BODY

5¾ (6½, 7)"

4 (4¼, 4½)"

20 (20½, 21)"

8 (8½, 9)"

12"

34 (37, 40)"

4-st rep

4

1

COLOR KEY

▨ MC

☐ CC

With MC, join yarn to upper sts and work in St st until pocket measures 3"/7.5cm. Bind off.

Pocket Trim

With MC, join yarn to lower sts and work in k1, p1 rib on the 20 sts for 4 rows. Bind off.
Sew sides and bottom of pocket to WS of vest. Sew edges of pocket trim in place.
Turn hem to WS along turning ridge and sew in place. Ω

Shuvee

Susanne Allen creates a look that's equally at home in the country or the city, with an oversize ribbed collar, wide ribbed bands, and a plush honeycomb cable pattern.

SIZES
Sized for Small, Medium, Large, X-Large, 1X, 2X. Shown in size Small.

FINISHED MEASUREMENTS
Bust (closed) 35 (38, 41, 43, 46, 49)"/89 (96.5, 104, 109, 117, 124.5)cm
Length 23 (23, 23½, 24, 24½, 25)"/58.5 (58.5, 59.5, 61, 62, 63.5)cm

MATERIALS
220 Superwash Aran by Cascade Yarns, 3½oz/100g hanks, each approx 150yd/137.5m (superwash merino wool)
- 7 (8, 9, 10, 10, 11) hanks in #873 extra crème cafe
- One pair size 8 (5mm) needles *or size to obtain gauge*
- Extra size 8 (5mm) needle for 3-needle bind-off
- Cable needle (cn)
- Stitch holders

GAUGE
24 sts and 24 rows to 4"/10cm over honeycomb cable pat using size 8 (5.5 mm) needles. *Take time to check gauge.*

STITCH GLOSSARY
4-st LC Sl 2 sts to cn and hold to *front*, k2, k2 from cn.
4-st RC Sl 2 sts to cn and hold to *back*, k2, k2 from cn.

3-NEEDLE BIND-OFF
1) Hold right sides of pieces together on 2 needles. Insert 3rd needle knitwise into first st of each needle, and wrap yarn knitwise.
2) Knit these 2 sts together, and slip them off the needles. *Knit the next 2 sts together in the same manner.
3) Slip first st on 3rd needle over 2nd st and off needle. Rep from * in step 2 across row until all sts are bound off.

HONEYCOMB CABLE PATTERN
(multiple of 8 sts plus 2)
Row 1 (RS) Knit.
Row 2 Purl.
Row 3 K1, *4-st RC, 4-st LC; rep from * to last st, k1.
Row 4 Purl.
Row 5 Knit.
Row 6 Purl.
Row 7 K1, *4-st LC, 4-st RC; rep from * to last st, k1.
Row 8 Purl.
Rep rows 1–8 for honeycomb cable pat.

BACK
Cast on 104 (112, 120, 128, 136, 144) sts.
Row 1 (RS) *K2, p2; rep from * to end.
Rep row 1 for k2, p2 rib for 2"/5cm.

Begin Honeycomb Cable Pat
Inc row 1 (RS) Kfb, k to last st, kfb—106 (114, 122, 130, 138, 146) sts.

Beg with pat row 2, work in honeycomb cable pat until piece measures 16"/40.5cm from beg, end with a pat row 7.

Shape Armhole

Next row (WS) Bind off 4 (4, 4, 4, 8, 8) sts, purl to end.

Pat row 1 (RS) Bind off 4 (4, 4, 4, 8, 8) sts, knit to end.

Pat row 2 (WS) Bind off 3 sts, p to end.

Pat row 3 (RS) Bind off 3 sts, k1, work in pat to last 2 sts, k2.

Pat row 4 Bind off 2 sts, p to end.

Pat row 5 Bind off 2 sts, k to end.

For sizes 1X and 2X only:

Cont to bind off 2 sts at beg of next 4 rows, keeping to pat as established.

For all sizes:

Work even in pat (with k1 selvage each side eliminated) on 88 (96, 104, 112, 104, 112) sts until armhole measures 7 (7, 7½, 8, 8½, 9)"/18 (18, 19, 20.5, 21.5, 23)cm. Place sts on holder.

LEFT FRONT

Cast on 48 (56, 56, 64, 64, 72) sts.

Row 1 (RS) *K2, p2; rep from * to end.

Rep row 1 for k2, p2 rib for 2"/5cm.

Begin Honeycomb Cable Pat

Inc row 1 (RS) Kfb, k to last st, kfb— 50 (58, 58, 66, 66, 74) sts.

Beg with pat row 2, work in honeycomb cable pat until piece measures 16"/40cm from beg, end with a pat row 8.

Shape Armhole

Next row (pat row 1, RS) Bind off 4 (4, 4, 4, 8, 8) sts, k to end.

Cont in pat as established, bind off 3 sts from armhole edge once, then 2 sts 1 (1, 1, 3, 3, 3) times—41 (49, 49, 53, 49, 57) sts.

Work even until armhole measures 3½ (3½, 4, 4½, 5, 5½)"/9 (9, 10, 11.5, 12.5, 14)cm, end with a RS row.

Shape Neck

Next row (WS) Bind off 7 (10, 7, 12, 7, 14) sts, p to end.
Cont to work in pat as established, bind off 2 (3, 2, 3, 2, 3) sts from neck edge 1 (1, 2, 1, 2, 1) times—30 (34, 36, 34, 36, 38) sts.
Neck dec row (RS) Work to last 3 sts, k2tog, k1.
Neck dec row (WS) P1, p2tog, p to end.
Rep these 2 dec rows once more—26 (30, 32, 34, 32, 34) sts.
Work even until armhole measures same as back. Then join shoulder sts tog with corresponding 26 (30, 32, 34, 32, 34) sts of back shoulder, using 3-needle bind-off method.

RIGHT FRONT

Work as for left front, reversing all shaping (by beg armhole shaping on WS pat row 8 and working neck dec rows as k1, SKP on the RS and p2tog tbl, p1 on the WS). When right front is completed, join shoulder tog as for left shoulder, leaving rem 36 (36, 40, 44, 40, 44) sts on holder for back neck.

FINISHING

Sew side seams.

Collar

Pick up and k 29 (31, 29, 35, 29, 35) sts from shaped right neck edge, k 36 (36, 40, 44, 40, 44) sts from back neck, pick up and k 29 (31, 29, 35, 29, 35) sts from shaped left neck edge—94 (98, 98, 114, 98, 114) sts.
Row 1 (WS) K2, *p2, k2; rep from * to end.
Cont in k2, p2 rib until collar measures 7"/18cm.
Bind off in rib.

Left Front Trim

Beg at neck edge, pick up and k 36 sts from collar and 122 (122, 126, 126, 130, 134) sts to lower edge—158 (158, 162, 162, 166, 170) sts.
Row 1 (WS) P2, *k2, p2; rep from * to end.
Work in rib for 2¼"/6cm. Bind off in rib.
Work right front trim in same manner. Ω

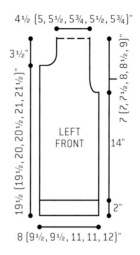

4½ (5, 5½, 5¾, 5½, 5¾)"

3½"

7 (7, 7½, 8, 8½, 9)"

LEFT FRONT

14"

19½ (19½, 20, 20½, 21, 21½)"

2"

8 (9½, 9½, 11, 11, 12)"

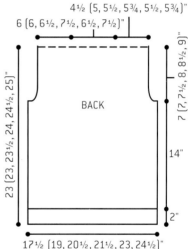

4½ (5, 5½, 5¾, 5½, 5¾)"

6 (6, 6½, 7½, 6½, 7½)"

7 (7, 7½, 8, 8½, 9)"

BACK

14"

23 (23, 23½, 24, 24½, 25)"

2"

17½ (19, 20½, 21½, 23, 24½)"

Princess Rooney

This sweet cropped waistcoat designed by **Valentina Devine** is all about texture, with an allover trinity stitch that provides both style and structure.

SIZES
Sized for Small, Medium, Large, X-Large. Shown in size Small.

FINISHED MEASUREMENTS
Bust (closed) 34 (37, 40, 43)"/86 (94, 104, 109)cm
Length (from center back) 13 (15, 15½, 17)"/33.5 (38.5, 39.5, 43.5)cm

MATERIALS
220 Superwash Aran by Cascade Yarns, 3½oz/100g hanks, each approx 150yd/137.5m (superwash merino wool)
- 3 (4, 4, 5) hanks in #1989 royal purple
- One pair size 8 (5mm) needles *or size to obtain gauge*
- Size D-3 (3.25mm) crochet hook
- Five ¾"/19mm ball buttons

GAUGE
22 sts and 22 rows to 4"/10cm over trinity st using size 8 (5mm) needles. *Take time to check gauge.*

TRINITY STITCH
(multiple of 4 sts plus 2)
Row 1 (WS) K1, *[k1, p1, k1] into next st, p3tog; rep from *, end k1.
Row 2 (RS) Purl.
Row 3 K1, *p3tog, [k1, p1, k1] into next st; rep from *, end k1.
Row 4 Purl.
Rep rows 1–4 for trinity st.

BACK
Cast on 94 (102, 110, 118) sts. Work in trinity st for 6 (7, 7, 8)"/15.5 (18, 18, 20.5)cm.

Shape Armhole
Bind off 4 sts at beg of next 2 rows. Dec 1 st each side every other row 4 times—78 (86, 94, 102) sts. Work even in pat until armhole measures 7 (8, 8½, 9)"/18 (20.5, 21.5, 23)cm, end with a RS row. Bind off knitwise on WS.

LEFT FRONT
Cast on 4 sts.
Row 1 (WS) K2, [k1, p1, k1] in next st, k1—6 sts.
Row 2 [K1, p1] in next st, p to end—7 sts.
Row 3 [K1, p1] in next st, [k1, p1, k1] in next st, p3tog, [k1, p1, k1] in next st, k1—10 sts.
Row 4 Rep row 2—1 st inc'd.
Row 5 [K1, p1] in next st; rep from * of row 1 of trinity st to last 2 sts, [k1, p1, k1] in next st, k1—3 sts inc'd.
Rep rows 4 and 5 until there are 46 (50 54, 58) sts, ending with a WS row.
Beg with a pat row 4, cont in trinity st until side edge measures same length as back to armhole, end with a WS row.

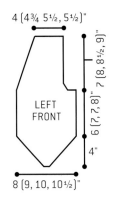

4 (4¾ 5½, 5½)"

LEFT FRONT

7 (8, 8½, 9)"

6 (7, 7, 8)"

4"

8 (9, 10, 10½)"

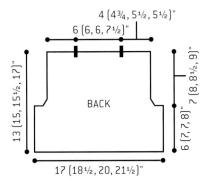

4 (4¾, 5½, 5½)"

6 (6, 6, 7½)"

BACK

13 (15, 15½, 17)"

7 (8, 8½, 9)"

6 (7, 7, 8)"

17 (18½, 20, 21½)"

Shape Armhole and Neck

Next row (RS) Bind off 4 sts, purl to end.
Cont in trinity st and work armhole decs as for back (beg of RS rows), AT THE SAME TIME, dec 1 st at neck edge (end of RS rows) every other row 16 (16, 16, 20) times—22 (26, 30, 30) sts. Work even until armhole measures same as back. Bind off rem sts for shoulder.

RIGHT FRONT

Work to correspond to left front, reversing armhole and neck shaping by working the first armhole bind-off at beg of a WS and dec sts at end of RS rows and work neck dec at beg of RS rows.

FINISHING

Sew shoulder and side seams. Place markers on left front for 5 buttons, the first one just above last inc row, the last one just below first neck dec and the other 3 spaced evenly between.

Crochet Edging

With RS facing and crochet hook, work 1 row sc evenly around outer edge of vest. Do not turn. Work 1 row backward sc (from left to right) in each sc, work ch-4 button loops on right front, opposite button markers. Fasten off.
Work in same way around each armhole edge.
Sew on buttons. Ω

Swingtime

Barb Brown gets playful with color blocking in this open vest with reversed fronts, graduated stripes on the back, and corrugated rib edgings.

SIZES
Sized for Small, Medium, Large, X-Large. Shown in size Small.

FINISHED MEASUREMENTS
Bust (closed) 32 (36, 40, 44)"/81 (91.5, 101.5, 111.5)cm
Length 22 (23, 23½, 24)"/56 (58.5, 59.5, 61)cm

MATERIALS
220 Superwash Aran by Cascade Yarns, 3½oz/100g hanks, each approx 150yd/137.5m (superwash merino wool)
- 2 (3, 4, 4) hanks in #900 light grey (A)
- 2 (2, 3, 3) hanks in #1994 silver grey (B)
- One each sizes 7 and 9 (4.5 and 5.5mm) circular needle, 24"/60cm long, *or size to obtain gauge*
- Spare size 9 (5.5mm) needle for 3-needle bind-off
- Stitch holders

GAUGE
16 sts and 24 rows to 4"/10cm over St st using larger needle. *Take time to check gauge.*

SHORT ROW WRAP AND TURN (W&T)
On RS row (on WS row)
1) Wyib (wyif), sl next st purlwise.
2) Move yarn between the needles to the front (back).

3) Sl the same st back to LH needle. Turn work. One st is wrapped.
4) When working the wrapped st, insert RH needle under the wrap and work it tog with the corresponding st on needle to close wraps.

3-NEEDLE BIND-OFF

1) Hold *right* sides of pieces together on 2 needles. Insert 3rd needle knitwise into first st of each needle, and wrap yarn knitwise.
2) Knit these 2 sts together, and slip them off the needles. *Knit the next 2 sts together in the same manner.
3) Slip first st on 3rd needle over 2nd st and off needle. Rep from * in step 2 across row until all sts are bound off.

CORRUGATED RIB

(over an odd number of sts)
Row 1 (WS) *K1 A, p1 B, rep from * to last st, k1 A.
Row 2 *P1 A, k1 B; rep from * to last st, p1 A.
Rep rows 1 and 2 for corrugated rib.

STRIPE SEQUENCE

Note Carry color not in use up the side of the work. In St st, work 1 row A, 2 rows B, 2 rows A, 3 rows B, 4 rows B, 4 rows A, 5 rows B, 5 rows A. Cont in this way, working 1 more row in each band. When an odd number of rows has been worked, slide sts to opposite end of needle to work next row, where the next color is waiting.

BACK

With A and smaller needle, cast on 63 (73, 79, 87) sts. Work in corrugated rib for 11 rows. Change to larger needle.
Next row (RS) With B, knit, inc 1 st across row— 64 (74, 80, 88) sts.
Work in stripe sequence until piece measures 15"/38cm from beg, end with a WS row.

Shape Armhole

Bind off 6 sts at beg of next 2 rows.
Next (dec) row (RS) K1, k2tog, k to last 3 sts, ssk, k1—2 sts dec'd.
Cont in St st and stripe pat and rep dec row every other row 1 (3, 4, 8) times more—48 (54, 58, 58) sts.

Cont in pat until armhole measures 6½ (7, 7½, 8)"/ 16.5 (18, 19, 20.5)cm, end with a WS row.

Shape Shoulders

Next row (RS) K to last 4 sts, w&t.
Next row (WS) P to last 4 sts, w&t.
Next row K to last 8 sts, w&t.
Next row P to last 8 sts, w&t.
Next row (RS) Knit all sts, closing wraps.
Place first and last 8 (11, 13, 13) sts on holders for shoulders.
Place center 32 sts on holder for back neck.

LEFT FRONT

With A and smaller needle, cast on 33 (37, 41, 45) sts. Work in corrugated rib as for back. Change to larger needle.
With B, work in St st until piece measures same as back to armhole, end with a WS row.

Shape Armhole

Next row (RS) Bind off 6 sts, k to end of row.
Purl 1 row.
Next (dec) row (RS) K1, ssk, k to end of row— 1 st dec'd.
Rep dec row every other row 1 (3, 4, 8) times more— 25 (27, 30, 30) sts.
Cont in St st until armhole measures 3 (3½, 4, 4½)"/7.5 (9, 10, 11.5)cm, end with a RS row.

Shape Neck

Next row (WS) Bind off 11 sts, p to end.
Next (dec) row (RS) K to last 3 sts, k2tog, k1— 1 st dec'd.
Rep dec row every other row 5 (4, 5, 5) times more— 8 (11, 13, 13) sts.
Work even until armhole measures 6½ (7, 7½, 8)"/ 16.5 (18, 19, 20.5)cm, end with a WS row.

Shape Shoulders

Next row (RS) Knit.

Next row P to last 4 sts, w&t.
Next row Knit.
Next row P to last 8 sts, w&t.
Next row Knit, closing wraps.
Place sts on st holder.

RIGHT FRONT

With A and smaller needle, cast on 33 (37, 41, 45) sts. Work in corrugated rib as for back. Change to larger needles.

With A, work as for left front to shoulder shaping, reversing all shaping by binding off for armhole at beg of WS rows and working armhole decs at end of row as k2tog, k1; binding off for neck at beg of RS row and working decs at beg of row as k1, ssk.

Shape Shoulders

Next row (RS) K to last 4 sts, w&t.
Next row Purl.
Next row K to last 8 sts, w&t.
Next row Purl, closing wraps.
Place sts on holder.

FINISHING

Join shoulders using 3-needle bind-off.
Sew side seams.

Neckband

With RS facing, smaller needle and B, pick up and k 39 sts along right front neck edge, k32 from back neck holder, pick up and k 38 sts along left front neck edge—109 sts.
Row 1 (WS) *K1 B, p1 A; rep from * to last st, k1 A.
Row 2 *P1 A, k1 B; rep from * to last st, p1 A.
Rep row 1. With B, bind off loosely in rib.

Armhole Trim

With RS facing, smaller needle and B, beg at side seam, pick up and k 80 (84, 88, 90) sts. Work as for neckband. Sew seam.

Left Front Band

With RS facing, smaller needle and A, pick up and k 109 (111, 113, 115) sts along left front edge.
Row 1 (WS) *P1, k1; rep from * to last st, p1.
Row 2 K the knit sts and p the purl sts.
Rep row 2 three times more for k1, p1 rib. Bind off loosely in rib.

Right Front Band

With RS facing, smaller needle and B, work as for left front band. Ω

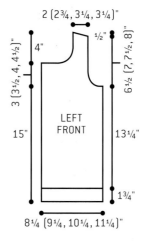

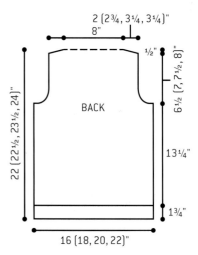

Genuine Risk

You'll be rewarded handsomely if you take on this pretty design by **Eulalia Choi**, featuring a two-color cable motif and contrasting curled edgings.

SIZES
Sized for Small, Medium, Large, 1X. Shown in size Small.

FINISHED MEASUREMENTS
Bust 32 (36, 40, 44)"/81 (91.5, 101.5, 111.5)cm
Length 27 (27, 27½, 28)"/66.5 (68.5, 70, 71)cm

MATERIALS
220 Superwash Aran by Cascade Yarns, 3½oz/100g hanks, each approx 150yd/137.5m (superwash merino wool)
- 5 (6, 7, 7) hanks in #855 maroon (A)
- 2 hanks in #893 ruby (B)
- 1 hank each in #900 charcoal (C) and #1946 silver grey (D)
- One each sizes 7, 8, and 9 (4.5, 5, and 5.5mm) circular needle, 24"/60cm long, *or size to obtain gauge*
- Cable needle (cn)
- Stitch markers
- Stitch holders

GAUGE
15 sts and 24 rows to 4"/10cm over garter st using size 9 (5.5mm) needle. *Take time to check gauge.*

STITCH GLOSSARY
4-st RC Sl 2 sts to cn and hold to *back*, k2, k2 from cn.
6-st RC Sl 3 sts to cn and hold to *back*, k3, k3 from cn.

6-st dec RC Sl 3 sts to cn and hold to *back*, k1, k2tog, k2tog, k1 from cn.

8-st RC Sl 4 sts to cn and hold to *back*, k4, k4 from cn.

8-st LC Sl 4 sts to cn and hold to *front*, k4, k4 from cn.

10-st dec RC Sl 5 sts to cn and hold to *back*, k1, k2tog, k2, then k2, k2tog, k1 from cn.

10-st dec LC Sl 5 sts to cn and hold to *front*, k1, k2tog, k2, then k2, k2tog, k1 from cn.

12-st RC Sl 6 sts to cn and hold to *back*, k6, k6 from cn.

12-st LC Sl 6 sts to cn and hold to *front*, k6, k6 from cn.

12-st dec RC Sl 6 sts to cn and hold to *back*, k4, k2tog, then k2tog, k4 from cn.

12-st dec LC Sl 6 sts to cn and hold to *front*, k4, k2tog, then k2tog, k4 from cn.

NOTES

1) Take length measurements at center, or longest part, of front and back.

2) Circular needles are used to accommodate large number of sts and chart 1 technique. Do not join.

BACK

Lower Trim

With size 8 (5mm) needle and A, cast on 120 (128, 140, 150) sts.

Begin Chart 1

Row 1a (RS) With B, work 2-st rep across. Do not turn work, slide sts to opposite end of needle to work next row from RS.

Row 1b (RS) With A, work 2-st rep across. Turn.

Row 2a (WS) With B, work 2-st rep across. Do not turn work, slide sts to opposite end of needle to work next row from WS.

Row 2b (WS) With A, work 2-st rep across.
Cont to work chart in this way through row 14b, noting that rows 6–11 are worked only once. Turn work before working these rows.
With A, bind off.

Beg Back Body

Fold upper edge of trim to RS. With size 9 (5.5mm) needle and A, working into the 3rd row of floats in A on WS of trim, pick up and k 91 (97, 105, 113) sts evenly across so that top of trim curls to RS of work. With A, purl 1 WS row.

Beg Chart 2

Row 1 (RS) K14 (17, 21, 25), place marker (pm), work 24-st chart rep twice, work to end of chart, pm, k to end.

Row 2 (WS) K to marker, work chart to rep line, work 24-st rep twice, k to end.

Cont to work chart in this way through row 38, then rep rows 25–38 once, then work rows 39–44, working sts outside of chart in garter st in A, AT THE SAME TIME, dec 1 st each side every 10th row twice—87 (93, 101, 109) sts.

Beg Chart 3

Note Read before cont to knit.

Work chart 3 between markers as before through row 20, AT THE SAME TIME, when piece measures 14"/35.5cm from beg, inc 1 st each side on next row, then every 6th row 4 times more—75 (81, 89, 97) sts when all shaping is complete (note that chart 4 will begin before shaping is complete).

Beg Chart 4

Note Cont to work shaping at side edges. Read before cont to knit.

Row 1 (RS) K to marker, work 16-st chart rep twice, work to end of chart, k to end.

Row 2 (WS) K to marker, work chart to rep line, work 16-st rep twice, k to end.

Cont to work chart 4 in this way through row 14, then rep rows 5–14 four times more, then rep rows 15–22 to end, AT THE SAME TIME, when piece measures 19"/48cm from beg, end with a WS row and shape armhole as foll:

Bind off 3 (3, 4, 5) sts at beg of next 2 rows, 2 (2, 3, 4)

sts at beg of next 2 rows. Dec 1 st each side on next row, then every other row 3 (4, 4, 4) times more— 57 (61, 65, 69) sts.

Work even, foll chart and maintaining sts outside of chart in garter st, until armhole measures 7 (7, 7½, 8)"/18 (18, 19, 20.5)cm, end with a WS row.

Shape Back Neck

Next row (RS) Work 13 (15, 17, 19) sts in pat, join 2nd ball of A and bind off center 31 sts, work to end. Working both sides at once, bind off 3 sts from each neck edge twice—7 (9, 11, 13) sts rem each side. Work even in pat until armhole measures 8 (8, 8½, 9)"/20.5 (20.5, 21.5, 23)cm. Bind off rem sts each side.

FRONT

Work as for back until armhole measures 0 (0,½, 1)"/ 0 (0, 1.5, 2.5)cm, end with a WS row and mark center st on last row.

Shape Front Neck

Next row (RS) Work in pat to center st, place center st on st holder, join 2nd ball of yarn and work to end.
Next row (WS) Work in pat.
Dec row 1 Working in pat, dec 1 st at each neck edge.
Row 2 (WS) Work in pat.
Dec row 3 Working in pat, dec 1 st at each neck edge.
Dec row 4 Working in pat, dec 1 st at each neck edge.
Rep last 4 rows 6 times more, AT THE SAME TIME, cont armhole shaping as for back—7 (9, 11, 13) sts rem when all shaping is complete. Work even until armhole measures same as back to shoulder, then work 4 rows more in pat. Bind off.

FINISHING

Block pieces lightly to measurements, do not block lower trim. Sew shoulder seams. Sew side seams.

Neck Trim

With RS facing, size 8 (5mm) needle, and A, beg at

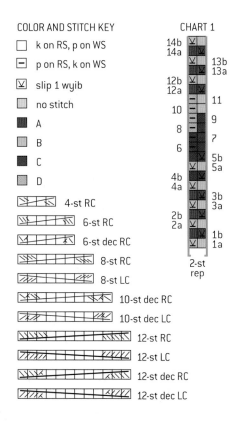

COLOR AND STITCH KEY

☐ k on RS, p on WS
☐ p on RS, k on WS
☑ slip 1 wyib
☐ no stitch
■ A
■ B
■ C
■ D

4-st RC
6-st RC
6-st dec RC
8-st RC
8-st LC
10-st dec RC
10-st dec LC
12-st RC
12-st LC
12-st dec RC
12-st dec LC

CHART 1

center front neck, pick up and p 43 sts along right front neck edge to shoulder, 52 sts along back neck edge, 42 sts along left front neck edge to center, place center st on holder on needle—138 sts. Turn to work a RS row. (Note that RS of edging will be WS of neck edge.)

Beg Chart 1

Row 1a (RS) With B, work 2-st rep to end. Do not turn, slide sts to opposite side of needle to work next row from RS.
Row 1b (RS) With A, work 2-st rep to end.
Cont to work chart 1 in this way through row 3b. With A, bind off. Edging will curl toward neck trim, with WS (purl) side showing along RS of neck.
With RS facing, size 8 (5mm) needle, and B, working behind curled edge into same picked-up sts, pick up and k 43 sts along right front neck edge to shoulder,

CHART 2

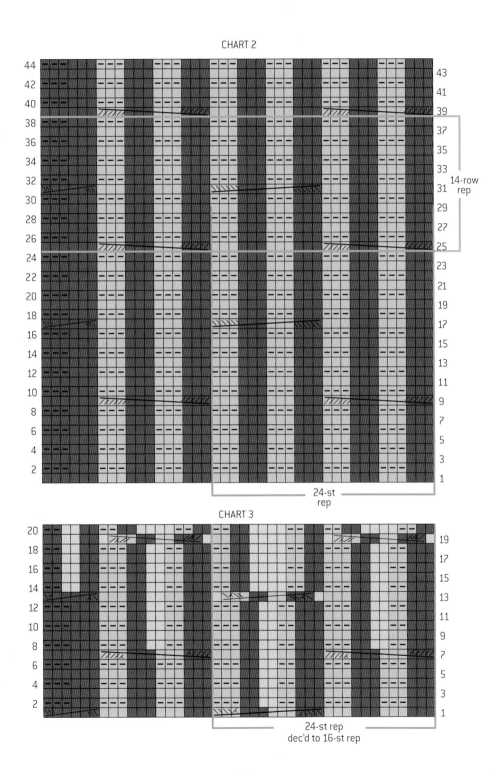

24-st
rep

14-row
rep

CHART 3

24-st rep
dec'd to 16-st rep

52 sts along back neck edge, 43 sts along left front neck edge to center front—138 sts. Do *not* turn, slide sts to opposite end of needle to work next row from RS. Beg with B and row 5a, cont to work chart 1 through row 14b. With A, bind off.

Overlap front edges of neck trim with right trim over left trim and sew side edges to neck edge.

Armhole Trim

With RS facing, size 8 (5mm) needle, and A, pick up and k 88 (88, 92, 98) sts evenly along armhole edge. Do not turn, slide sts to opposite end of needle to work next row from RS. (Note that RS of armhole trim will be RS of armhole edge.)

Work rows 1a–3b of chart 1. With A, bind off. Edging will curl toward body, with WS (purl side) showing. With RS facing, size 8 (5mm) needle, and B, working behind curled edge into same picked-up sts, pick up and k 88 (88, 92, 98) sts evenly along armhole edge.

Next row (WS) With A, *k1, p1; rep from * to end.

With C, work 2 rows in k1, p1 rib as established.

Next row (RS) *With D, k1, with C, p1; rep from * to end.

Next row (WS) *With C, k1, with D, p1; rep from * to end.

Change to size 7 (4.5mm) needle. Working in k1, p1 rib, work 1 row in A, then 1 row in B. With A, bind off in rib. Sew trim seam. Ω

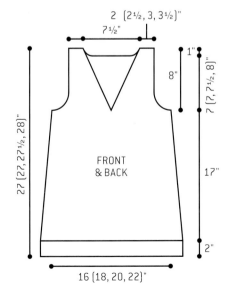

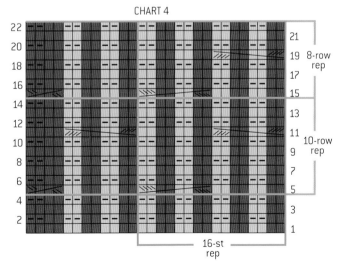

CHART 4

Summer Guest

Columns of leaf lace, a turned hem, and waist shaping make this scoopneck vest by **Kim Haesemeyer** an elegant layer for brisk summer days.

SIZES
Sized for X-Small, Small, Medium, Large, 1X. Shown in size X-Small.

FINISHED MEASUREMENTS
Bust 32½ (36¼, 40, 43¾, 47½)"/82.5 (92, 101.5, 111, 120.5)cm
Length 20½ (21, 21½, 22, 22½)"/52 (53.5, 54.5, 56, 57)cm

MATERIALS
220 Superwash Aran by Cascade Yarns, 3½oz/100g hanks, each approx 150yd/137.5m (superwash merino wool)
- 4 (4, 5, 5, 6) hanks in #845 denim
- One each sizes 7 and 9 (4.5 and 5.5mm) circular needle, each 24"/60cm long, *or size to obtain gauge*
- Size 7 (4.5mm) circular needle, 16"/40cm long
- Size 7 (4.5mm) crochet hook
- Stitch markers
- Stitch holders
- Scrap yarn

GAUGE
17 sts and 24 rows/rnds to 4"/10cm over St st using larger needles. *Take time to check gauge.*

PROVISIONAL CAST-ON
Using scrap yarn and crochet hook, ch the number of sts to cast on plus a few extra. Cut a tail and pull the tail through the last chain. With knitting needle and yarn, pick up and knit the stated number of sts through the "purl bumps" on the back of the chain. To remove scrap yarn chain, when instructed, pull out the tail from the last crochet stitch. Gently and slowly pull on the tail to unravel the crochet stitches, carefully placing each released knit stitch on a needle.

3-NEEDLE BIND-OFF
1) Hold right sides of pieces together on 2 needles. Insert 3rd needle knitwise into first st of each needle, and wrap yarn knitwise.
2) Knit these 2 sts together, and slip them off the needles. *Knit the next 2 sts together in the same manner.
3) Slip first st on 3rd needle over 2nd st and off needle. Rep from * in step 2 across row until all sts are bound off.

STITCH GLOSSARY
M1R Insert LH needle from back to front under the strand between last st worked and next st on LH needle. K into the front loop to twist the st.
M1L Insert LH needle from front to back under the strand between last st worked and next st on LH needle. K into the back loop to twist the st.

NOTE
Vest is worked in the round to the underarm, then worked back and forth to shoulder.

BODY

With longer size 7 (4.5mm) circular needle and using provisional cast-on method, cast on 146 (162, 178, 194, 210) sts. Join and place marker (pm) for beg of rnd. Work in St st (k every rnd) for 2½"/6.5cm. Switch to larger needle. Purl 1 rnd for turning rnd. Knit 1 rnd.

Begin Chart

Next rnd *K8 (10, 12, 14, 16), pm, [work chart over 11 sts, pm, k12 (14, 16, 18, 20), pm] twice, work chart over 11 sts, pm, k8 (10, 12, 14, 16)*, pm for side seam, rep from * to * once more.

Work in pat as established until piece measures 2½"/6.5cm from turning rnd, end with an odd-number chart rnd. Carefully remove scrap yarn from provisional cast-on and place sts on smaller circular needle. Fold hem to WS along turning rnd so that needles are parallel.

Next (hem joining) rnd *Knit 1 st from larger needle tog with 1 st from provisional cast-on; rep from * around.

Next (dec) rnd [K1, k2tog, work in pat to 3 sts before side marker, ssk, k1] twice—4 sts dec'd.

Rep dec rnd every 6th rnd 5 times more—122 (138, 154, 170, 186) sts.

Work even in pat until piece measures approx 7"/18cm from turning row.

Next (inc) rnd [K to first chart panel, work first chart panel, k1, M1L, k to center chart panel, work center chart panel, k to 1 st before 3rd chart panel, M1R, k1, work 3rd chart panel, k to marker] twice—4 sts inc'd.

Rep inc rnd every 8th rnd 3 times more—138 (154, 170, 186, 202) sts.

Work even until 14 rnds of chart have been worked 5 times from beg, then rep rnds 1–8 once more, end last rnd 4 (4, 5, 5, 6) sts before beg-of-rnd marker. Piece measures approx 13½"/34.5cm from turning row.

Divide for Front and Back

Note Discontinue chart pat on front, and cont chart only over center chart panel on back. Work rem sts in St st.

Next rnd Bind off 8 (8, 10, 10, 12) sts, k to 4 (4, 5, 5, 6) sts before side marker, bind off 8 (8, 10, 10, 12) sts, k to end. Turn to work back and forth.

Next row (WS) P61 (69, 75, 83, 89) for back, turn, leaving rem 61 (69, 75, 83, 89) sts on st holder for front.

Shape Back Armhole

Dec row (RS) K1, k2tog, work to last 3 sts, ssk, k1—2 sts dec'd.

Rep dec row every other row 2 (3, 4, 5, 5) times, then every 4th row 3 (4, 4, 4, 5) times—49 (53, 57, 63, 67) sts.

Work even until until 14 rnds/rows of chart have been worked 7 times over center chart panel, then work rows 1–8 once more. Work all sts in St st until armhole measures 5¼ (5¾, 6¼, 6¾, 7¼)"/13.5 (14.5, 16, 17, 18.5)cm, end with a WS row and mark center 11 (11, 11, 13, 13) sts on last row.

Shape Back Neck

Next row (RS) K to center marked sts, join 2nd ball of yarn and bind off center 11 (11, 11, 13, 13) sts, k to end.

Working both sides at once, bind off 5 sts from each neck edge once, then dec 1 st at each neck edge every row 5 times—9 (11, 13, 15, 17) sts rem each side. Place sts each side on st holder.

Front

Note Read before cont to knit. For size Small only, neck shaping begins at same time as armhole shaping.

Return to sts on hold for front. Join yarn, ready to work a WS row.

Next row (WS) Purl. Mark center 11 (11, 11, 13, 13) sts. Beg armhole shaping as for back, AT THE SAME TIME, when armhole measures 0 (½, 1, 1½, 2)"/0 (1.5, 2.5, 4, 5)cm, end with a WS row and work front neck shaping as foll:

Next row (RS) Work to center marked sts, join 2nd ball of yarn, bind off center 11 (11, 11, 13, 13) sts, work to end.

Cont armhole shaping as for back and, working both sides at once, bind off 5 sts from each neck edge once, then dec 1 st at each neck edge every other row

5 times—9 (11, 13, 15, 17) sts rem when all shaping is complete.

Work even until armhole measures same as back to shoulder. Place sts each side on st holder.

FINISHING

Join shoulders using 3-needle bind-off.

Neck Edging

With RS facing and shorter size 7 (4.5mm) circular needle, pick up and k 116 (116, 116, 120, 120) sts evenly around neck edge. Join and pm for beg of rnd.
Rnd 1 *K2, p2; rep from * to end.
Rep rnd 1 for k2, p2 rib for 1"/2.5cm. Bind off in rib.

Armhole Edging

With RS facing and shorter size 7 (4.5mm) circular needle, pick up and k 68 (72, 76, 84, 88) sts evenly around armhole edge. Work 4 rnds in k2, p2 rib. Bind off in rib. ♘

STITCH KEY
☐ k on RS, p on WS
☒ k2tog
☒ SSK
⊙ yo
⩒ S2KP

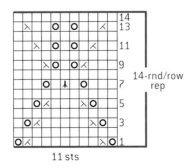

11 sts

14-rnd/row rep

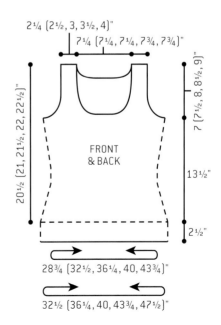

2¼ (2½, 3, 3½, 4)"

7¼ (7¼, 7¼, 7¾, 7¾)"

7 (7½, 8, 8½, 9)"

20½ (21, 21½, 22, 22½)"

FRONT & BACK

13½"

2½"

28¾ (32½, 36¼, 40, 43¾)"

32½ (36¼, 40, 43¾, 47½)"

Tools & Techniques

ABBREVIATIONS

approx	approximately	**M1 p-st**	make one purl stitch (see glossary)	**S2KP**	slip 2 stitches together, knit 1, pass 2 slip stitches over knit 1
beg	begin(ning)				
CC	contrasting color	**M1R**	make one right (see glossary)	**sc**	single crochet
ch	chain			**sl**	slip
cm	centimeter(s)	**oz**	ounce(s)	**sl st**	slip stitch
cn	cable needle	**p**	purl	**spp**	slip, purl, pass sl st over
cont	continu(e)(ing)	**pfb**	purl into front and back of a stitch—one stitch has been increased	**ssk (ssp)**	slip 2 sts knitwise one at a time, insert LH needle through fronts of sts and knit (purl) together
dec	decreas(e)(ing)				
dpn(s)	double-pointed needle(s)				
foll	follow(s)(ing)	**pat(s)**	pattern(s)	**sssk**	slip 3 sts one at a time knitwise, insert LH needle through fronts of sts and knit together
g	gram(s)	**pm**	place marker		
inc	increas(e)(ing)	**psso**	pass slip stitch(es) over		
k	knit	**p2tog**	purl two stitches together—one stitch has been decreased	**st(s)**	stitch(es)
kfb	knit into the front and back of a stitch—one stitch has been increased			**St st**	stockinette stitch
		rem	remain(s)(ing)	**tbl**	through back loop(s)
		rep	repeat	**tog**	together
k2tog	knit 2 stitches together—one stitch has been decreased	**RH**	right-hand	**WS**	wrong side(s)
		RS	right side(s)	**wyib**	with yarn in back
LH	left-hand	**rnd(s)**	round(s)	**wyif**	with yarn in front
lp(s)	loop(s)	**SKP**	slip 1, knit 1, pass slip stitch over—one stitch has been decreased	**yd(s)**	yd(s)
m	meter(s)			**yo**	yarn over needle
mm	millimeter(s)			*****	repeat directions following * as indicated
MC	main color	**SK2P**	slip 1, knit 2 together, pass slip stitch over the k2tog—two stitches decreased		
M1 or M1L	make one or make one left (see glossary)			**[ ]**	repeat directions inside brackets as indicated

SKILL LEVELS

Beginner

Ideal first project.

Easy

Basic stitches, minimal shaping, and simple finishing.

Intermediate

For knitters with some experience. More intricate stitches, shaping, and finishing.

Experienced

For knitters able to work patterns with complicated shaping and finishing.

METRIC CONVERSIONS

To convert from inches to centimeters, simply multiply by 2.54.

GAUGE

Make a test swatch at least 4"/10cm square. If the number of stitches and rows does not correspond to the gauge given, you must change the needle size. An easy rule to follow is: To get fewer stitches to the inch/cm, use a larger needle; to get more stitches to the inch/cm, use a smaller needle. Continue to try different needle sizes until you get the same number of stitches in the gauge.

KNITTING NEEDLES

U.S.	Metric	U.S.	Metric
0	2mm	9	5.5mm
1	2.25mm	10	6mm
2	2.75mm	10½	6.5mm
3	3.25mm	11	8mm
4	3.5mm	13	9mm
5	3.75mm	15	10mm
6	4mm	17	12.75mm
7	4.5mm	19	15mm
8	5mm	35	19mm

GLOSSARY

bind off Used to finish an edge or segment. Lift the first stitch over the second, the second over the third, etc. (U.K.: cast off)

bind off in rib or pat Work in rib or pat as you bind off. (Knit the knit stitches, purl the purl stitches.)

cast on Place a foundation row of stitches upon the needle in order to begin knitting.

decrease Reduce the stitches in a row (for example, knit two together).

increase Add stitches in a row (for example, knit in front and back of stitch).

knitwise Insert the needle into the stitch as if you were going to knit it.

make one or make one left Insert left-hand needle from front to back under the strand between last st worked and next st on left-hand needle. Knit into the back loop to twist the stitch.

make one p-st Insert needle from front to back under the strand between the last stitch worked and the next stitch on the left-hand needle. Purl into the back loop to twist the stitch.

make one right Insert left-hand needle from back to front under the strand between the last stitch worked and the next stitch on left-hand needle. Knit into the front loop to twist the stitch.

no stitch On some charts, "no stitch" is indicated with shaded spaces where stitches have been decreased or not yet made. In such cases, work the stitches of the chart, skipping over the "no stitch" spaces.

place marker Place or attach a loop of contrast yarn or purchased stitch marker as indicated.

pick up and knit (purl) Knit (or purl) into the loops along an edge.

purlwise Insert the needle into the stitch as if you were going to purl it.

selvage stitch Edge stitch that helps make seaming easier.

slip, slip, knit Slip next two stitches knitwise, one at a time, to right-hand needle. Insert tip of left-hand needle into fronts of these stitches, from left to right. Knit them together. One stitch has been decreased.

slip, slip, slip, knit Slip next three stitches knitwise, one at a time, to right-hand needle. Insert tip of left-hand needle into fronts of these stitches, from left to right. Knit them together. Two stitches have been decreased.

slip stitch An unworked stitch made by passing a stitch from the left-hand to the right-hand needle as if to purl.

work even Continue in pattern without increasing or decreasing. (U.K.: work straight)

yarn over Make a new stitch by wrapping the yarn over the right-hand needle. (U.K.: yfwd, yon, yrn)

STANDARD YARN WEIGHTS TABLE
Categories of yarn, gauge ranges, and recommended needle and hook sizes

Yarn Weight Symbol & Category Names	0 Lace	1 Super Fine	2 Fine	3 Light	4 Medium	5 Bulky	6 Super Bulky
Type of Yarns in Category	Fingering 10 count crochet thread	Sock, Fingering, Baby	Sport, Baby	DK, Light Worsted	Worsted, Afghan, Aran	Chunky, Craft, Rug	Bulky, Roving
Knit Gauge Range* in Stockinette Stitch to 4 inches	33–40** sts	27–32 sts	23–26 sts	21–24 sts	16–20 sts	12–15 sts	6–11 sts
Recommended Needle in Metric Size Range	1.5–2.25 mm	2.25–3.25 mm	3.25–3.75 mm	3.75–4.5 mm	4.5–5.5 mm	5.5–8 mm	8 mm and larger
Recommended Needle U.S. Size Range	000 to 1	1 to 3	3 to 5	5 to 7	7 to 9	9 to 11	11 and larger
Crochet Gauge* Ranges in Single Crochet to 4 inch	32–42 double crochets**	21–32 sts	16–20 sts	12–17 sts	11–14 sts	8–11 sts	5–9 sts
Recommended Hook in Metric Size Range	Steel*** 1.6–1.4mm Regular hook 2.25 mm	2.25–3.5 mm	3.5–4.5 mm	4.5–5.5 mm	5.5–6.5 mm	6.5–9 mm	9 mm and larger
Recommended Hook U.S. Size Range	Steel*** 6, 7, 8 Regular hook B–1	B–1 to E–4	E–4 to 7	7 to I–9	I–9 to K–10½	K–10½ to M–13	M–13 and larger

* Guidelines only: The above reflect the most commonly used gauges and needle or hook sizes for specific yarn categories.
** Lace weight yarns are usually knitted or crocheted on larger needles and hooks to create lacy, openwork patterns. Accordingly, a gauge range is difficult to determine. Always follow the gauge stated in your pattern.
*** Steel crochet hooks are sized differently from regular hooks—the higher the number, the smaller the hook, which is the reverse of regular hook sizing.

THREE-NEEDLE BIND-OFF

This bind-off is used to join two edges that have the same number of stitches, such as shoulder edges, which have been placed on holders.

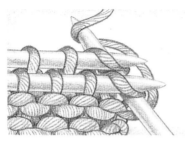

1. With the right side of the two pieces facing each other, and the needles parallel, insert a third needle knitwise into the first stitch of each needle. Wrap the yarn around the needle as if to knit.

2. Knit these two stitches together and slip them off the needles. *Knit the next two stitches together in the same way as shown.

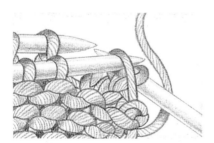

3. Slip the first stitch on the third needle over the second stitch and off the needle. Repeat from the * in step 2 across the row until all the stitches are bound off.

PICKING UP STITCHES ALONG A VERTICAL EDGE

Stitches picked up along a side edge.

1. Insert the knitting needle into the corner stitch of the first row, one stitch in from the side edge. Wrap the yarn around the needle knitwise.

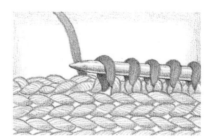

2. Draw the yarn through. You have picked up one stitch. Continue to pick up stitches along the edge. Occasionally skip one row to keep the edge from flaring.

SHORT ROW SHAPING: "WRAP & TURN"

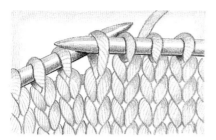

1. To prevent holes in the piece and create a smooth transition, wrap a knit stitch as follows: With the yarn in back, slip the next stitch purlwise.

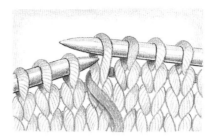

2. Move the yarn between the needle to the front of the work.

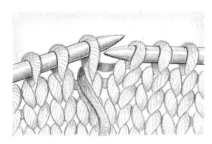

3. Slip the same stitch back to the left needle. Turn the work, bringing the yarn to the purl side between the needles. One stitch is wrapped.

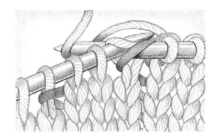

4. When you have completed all the short rows, you must hide the wraps. Work to just before the wrapped stitch. Insert the right needles under the wrap and knitwise into the wrapped stitch. Knit them together.

YARN OVERS

Between two knit stitches Bring the yarn from the back of the work to the front between the two needles. Knit the next stitch, bringing the yarn to the back over the right-hand needle, as shown.

Between two purl stitches Leave the yarn at the front of the work. Bring the yarn to the back over the right-hand needle and to the front again, as shown. Purl the next stitch.

Index